The Edinburgh Companion to
James Kelman

Edinburgh Companions to Scottish Literature

Series Editors: Ian Brown and Thomas Owen Clancy

The Edinburgh Companion to James Kelman

Edited by Scott Hames

Edinburgh University Press

© in this edition Edinburgh University Press, 2010
© in the individual contributions is retained by the authors

Edinburgh University Press Ltd
22 George Square, Edinburgh

www.euppublishing.com

Typeset in 10.5 on 12.5pt Goudy
by Servis Filmsetting Ltd, Stockport, Cheshire, and
printed and bound in Great Britain by
CPI Antony Rowe, Chippenham and Eastbourne

A CIP record for this book is available from the British Library

ISBN 978 0 7486 3963 2 (hardback)
ISBN 978 0 7486 3964 9 (paperback)

The right of Scott Hames to be identified as editor
and of the contributors to be identified as authors of
this work has been asserted in accordance with
the Copyright, Designs and Patents Act 1988.

Contents

Series Editors' Preface

The preface to this series' initial tranche of volumes recognised that some literary canons can conceive of a single 'Great Tradition'. The series editors consider that there is no such simple way of conceiving of Scottish literature's variousness. This arises from a multilingual and multivalent culture. It also arises from a culture that includes authors who move for many different reasons beyond Scotland's physical boundaries, sometimes to return, sometimes not. The late Iain Wright in *The Edinburgh History of Scottish Literature* talked of the Scots as a 'semi-nomadic people'. Robert Louis Stevenson travelled in stages across the world; Muriel Spark settled in Southern Africa, England and then Italy; James Kelman, while remaining close to his roots in Glasgow, has spent important periods in the United States; Irvine Welsh has moved from Leith, in Edinburgh, to a series of domestic bases on both sides of the Atlantic.

All four writers at one time and in one way or another have been under-appreciated. Stevenson – most notoriously perhaps – for a time was seen as simply an adventure writer for the young. Yet Stevenson is now recognised not for simplicity, but his wonderful complexity, an international writer whose admirers included Borges and Nabokov. Similarly, the other three have firm international reputations based on innovation, literary experiment and pushing formal boundaries. All have grown out of the rich interrelationship of English and Scots in the literature to which they contribute; they embody its intercultural richness, hybridity and cosmopolitan potential. Some of their subject matter is far-flung; often they are situated not only physically but also in literary terms well beyond Scotland. Yet they are all important contributors to Scottish literature, a fact which problematises in the most positive and creative way any easy notion of what Scottish literature is.

Ian Brown
Thomas Owen Clancy

Brief Biography of James Kelman

James Kelman was born in Glasgow in 1946. Leaving school at the earliest opportunity, he began a six-year apprenticeship as a compositor (type-setter) aged 15. Kelman's family briefly emigrated to California in 1963–4. On returning to Britain, he worked a variety of jobs including bus driving in Glasgow, farm work in the Channel Islands, asbestos-sheet mixing in Manchester and construction labouring in London. He began writing aged 22 while in London, where he met and married Marie Connors from Swansea. The couple returned in 1970 to Glasgow, where Kelman attended extramural classes in creative writing run by Philip Hobsbaum from 1971 to 1972. His debut story collection *An Old Pub Near the Angel* was first published in Maine in 1973; Kelman was thus a published writer before beginning, in 1975, a degree in English and Philosophy at Strathclyde University. Kelman has been a creative writing tutor at Goldsmiths College (London), the University of Texas-at-Austin, and San José State University, California. With Tom Leonard and Alasdair Gray, he held the Chair of Creative Writing for a short period at the University of Glasgow. He is also a dramatist and has written for stage, film and radio. He and his wife live in Glasgow, not far from their two daughters and two grandchildren.

Publishing Chronology

1973   *An Old Pub Near the Angel* (stories)
1976   *Three Glasgow Writers* (with Alex Hamilton and Tom Leonard; stories)
1978   *Short Tales from the Night Shift* (stories)
1983   *Not not while the giro* (stories)
1984   *The Busconductor Hines* (novel)
1985   *A Chancer* (novel)*
1985   *Lean Tales* (with Agnes Owens and Alasdair Gray; stories)
1987   *Greyhound for Breakfast* (stories)

1989 *A Disaffection* (novel)
1991 *The Burn* (stories)
1991 *Hardie & Baird and Other Plays* (plays)
1992 *Some Recent Attacks: Essays Cultural and Political* (essays)
1994 *How late it was, how late* (novel)
1998 *The Good Times* (stories)
2001 *Translated Accounts* (novel)
2002 *"And the judges said . . .": Essays* (essays)
2004 *You Have to be Careful in the Land of the Free* (novel)
2008 *Kieron Smith, boy* (novel)
2010 *If it is your life* (stories)**

* *A Chancer* was Kelman's first novel, but *The Busconductor Hines* was published earlier.
** published after this book was written.

Awards

Cheltenham Prize for Literature (1987), James Tait Black Memorial Prize (1989), Booker Prize and Writers' Guild Award for Best Fiction (1994), Scotland on Sunday/Glenfiddich Spirit of Scotland Award and Stakis Prize for Scottish Writer of the Year (1998), Scottish Arts Council/SMIT Book of the Year Award, Aye Write Prize and Saltire Award (2009). Shortlisted for 1989 Booker Prize and 2009 Man Booker International Prize.

Introduction

Scott Hames

James Kelman is probably the most important Scottish writer now living; certainly he is the most influential and acclaimed. And yet introducing him as a 'Scottish writer' already begins to shape our response to his work, in ways that are potentially limiting and simplistic. (To be sure, calling him 'important' and 'acclaimed' exerts another pressure.) Kelman's fiction is obsessed with such pitfalls of description, and often loops back on itself to question names, labels and first impressions, paring away received bias to get at the thing itself. His art declares war on stereotypes, but is saddled with plenty of its own. For the sake of accuracy as well as brevity, the unadorned facts of Kelman's life and career appear separately as 'A Brief Biography'. But how to describe Kelman's writing, which so often demands to know *by what right* and *from whose perspective* representation takes place?

We can begin by considering how this theme *within* Kelman's fiction relates to the real-world debates surrounding it. For example, this series of *Edinburgh Companions* locates Kelman within the field of Scottish Literature. Is this where he belongs? The day I began this Introduction, the following headline appeared on a newspaper website: 'James Kelman launches broadside against Scotland's literary culture'.[1] Shifting metaphors from warfare to divorce a few days later, another paper breathlessly reported 'Literary Scotland torn apart over Kelman spat'.[2]

The trigger for this latest 'spat', Kelman's thinly veiled rubbishing of Ian Rankin and J. K. Rowling ('if the Nobel Prize came from Scotland they would give it to a writer of fucking detective fiction, or [. . .] writing about some upper middle-class young magician'[3]) highlights a tension involved in any attempt to define 'Scottish Literature', or to situate a writer like Kelman within it. Do even the shoddiest genre novels qualify, so long as they are 'reflective of Scottish origins and experience'?[4] Classifying literary works simply according to nationality seems to mean placing Harry Potter alongside Walter Scott – both came from Edinburgh, after all.[5] Kelman's highly politicised work cannot be comfortably mounted within a national canon defined in these terms (namely, in his words, 'praise the mediocre'[6]). And yet he is perhaps *the* major influence on the younger generation of writers (Irvine Welsh, Janice Galloway, Alan Warner, A. L. Kennedy, Duncan McLean, Alan Bissett, for example) who have made recent Scottish writing so compelling – and so easy to describe, complacently, as a 'new renaissance' reflecting national confidence. Kelman is allergic to 'national confidence'; his success at home makes it all the more difficult to locate him there.

But shifting scenes only gives rise to another irony. Earlier in 2009 Kelman was nominated for the Man Booker International Prize, which recognises 'one writer's overall contribution to fiction on the world stage'.[7] His fellow nominees included Mario Vargas Llosa, Peter Carey, V. S. Naipaul, Joyce Carol Oates, Ngugi Wa Thiong'O and Alice Munro (the eventual winner). Paradoxically, Kelman's international profile is that of an uncompromising Scottish defender of the local, struggling fiercely against the dominance of metropolitan values. This localism is central to his cosmopolitan appeal; Kelman's innovative use of Glasgow English is a key reason why his work has been translated (with some difficulty) into a dozen languages ranging from Spanish to Serbian.[8] His sometimes belligerent insistence on the validity of 'marginal' working-class culture has brought him to the very centre of 'the world stage'. As the novelist Jonathan Coe once observed, Kelman is 'engaged in a long-standing struggle against the very values' by which his work is celebrated, insisting absolutely on its *own* criteria and authority.[9] There is a sense in which Kelman refuses to belong to any literary club which would accept him as a member.

Where does this leave his Scottishness? Kelman's defiant Booker Prize acceptance speech of 1994 – 'my culture and my language have the right to exist, and no one has the authority to dismiss that right' – was interpreted by some as a claim of right for Scottish literature.[10] And so Kelman became famous for defending a Scottish literary culture he now uses his global stature to 'tear apart' on its home turf? This bald contradiction tells us more about Kelman's critical reception than his art, and should redirect our attention accordingly. We could fill a *Journalist's Companion to James Kelman* five times the size of this book with lazy comparisons and manufactured controversies; few writers with a seat booked on 'the world stage' can have served as fodder for so many brainless column inches. The caricature of grim, foul-mouthed, 'chippy' Kelman is in perpetual danger of overshadowing his art, even to the point of travestying it.

Like its combative author, Kelman's prose relentlessly questions authority, interrogates the criteria by which it is praised, refuses to 'settle' into preconceived critical slots. The point is that we cannot easily get a 'fix' on Kelman without distorting what we mean to describe, or narrowing what we mean to explore. The chapters of this *Companion* have a different aim: to explain and illuminate Kelman's work, while respecting its disrespect for simplicity.

Overview of Companion

In 2001 the critic Drew Milne observed that 'the literary modernism of James Kelman's work has been obscured by critical emphases on
its Scottishness or on its representation of language as it is spoken in
Glasgow.'[11] It would be fair to say this emphasis has been reversed in recent
years. A glance at the index of this book will reveal a stronger focus on
Kelman's modernist influences than earlier figures in the Scottish literary
tradition, and more attention to textual experiments than local accents.
This is not to 'de-nationalise' Kelman's work; as Michael Gardiner's
chapter explains, it is simply that Kelman's affiliations and influences tend
to cut *across* peripheral traditions, rather than clustering around established canons. This being said, Kelman's continuing interest in Scottish
radical history, and his continuing, forceful influence on younger writers,
ensure the Scottish context will remain important for understanding his
work. (Indeed, being denounced as both 'Stalinist' and 'parochial' for his
criticisms of fellow Scottish writers creates an unlikely parallel with Hugh
MacDiarmid.[12]) Cairns Craig, who has most successfully located Kelman in
a Scottish tradition of the novel, turns in his chapter to the more specific
confines of Glasgow, where the archetypal Kelman protagonist is both lin-
guistically rooted and imprisoned.

Readers familiar with the city will know that Kelman's Glasgow is, in some
respects, anachronistic. His fiction rarely acknowledges the smart restau-
rants and festival of shopping which have usurped the central cityscape of
A Chancer or *The Busconductor Hines*.[13] In Kelman's Glasgow the poor still
live mainly in tenements, rather than tower blocks, and working men wear
boilersuits to mind-numbing factory jobs. There are no tracksuits, no call
centres, no American fast food and no Buckfast tonic wine. Young men hang
around snooker halls, rather than the multiplex; no one has a mobile phone
or a credit card, or partakes of any substance stronger than whisky. There are
'keelies' but no 'neds'. This can be explained as the author's scrupulous refusal
to judge working-class culture by alien criteria; others will ask if Kelman's
notion of working-class culture still exists.

His polemical activity shows a similar pattern. The recent *Guardian* report
of Kelman's 'astonishing outburst' at the Edinburgh Book Festival could,
in truth, have appeared in any of the past thirty years. In 2002 Kelman
published a rant-essay dating from 1987 called 'Shouting at the Edinburgh
Fringe Forum'; it begins by noting that he first tasted bile at the 'sham'
Festival in 1978. The 2009 story finds Kelman bemoaning the derisive treatment of 'contemporary' writing at the Festival, but his criticisms are hardly
fresh. It sometimes seems that Kelman's arguments and resentments never
change; to some this suggests a noble steadfastness of principle, to others a

dreary unwillingness to notice changing conditions and shifting political priorities.

This is one reason why it is difficult to 'periodise' Kelman's work, to divide it into eras marking clear stages of development. Chapters by Paul Shanks and Peter Boxall sketch out a provisional contrast between 'early' and 'recent' Kelman, and document a continuity of formal experiment, with evolving aims and methods. Between these chapters, Mary McGlynn examines the circuit of literary value in which *How late it was, how late* was both elevated and depreciated during the infamous Booker Prize controversy, and contrasts its reception with Kelman's earlier Booker-shortlisted novel, *A Disaffection*. Shifting our attention to literary form, Adrian Hunter's chapter orients Kelman's work to a specific tradition in the short story, identifying key influences and techniques and suggesting the shorter form may be Kelman's most accommodating medium. Mia Carter's chapter explores the strength, breadth and intimacy of Kelman's polemical writing, but also registers its frustrations, dissonance and sense of being 'closed' to alternative perspectives. David Archibald rounds off the 'Literary Forms' section of the book in a chapter documenting Kelman's dramatic work for stage, radio and screen, a story with a false start for every good review, but which presently looks set to bear cinematic fruit.

The second section of the book explores 'Critical Contexts' for Kelman's work, beginning with questions of locality, language and Scottishness. In charting Kelman's philosophical affinity with Noam Chomsky, Cairns Craig's chapter illuminates the link between language, freedom and creativity which is fundamental to Kelman's project. My own chapter offers an alternative perspective on Kelman's language, intended to challenge his close association with realist verisimilitude and 'straight' cultural representation. Michael Gardiner's chapter links Kelman to transnational and postcolonial writing, highlighting formal and political parallels with a range of writers from 'minor' and marginalised cultures. Carole Jones deconstructs the 'masculinism' of Kelman's fiction by examining the curious role of his female characters (as ciphers of traditional 'male' qualities) and his arguably gendered approach to narrating the self. Finally, Laurence Nicoll lucidly illustrates the direct influence of existential writers and thinkers on Kelman's fiction, and Kelman's failure, as a polemicist, to live by the rule-book of technique he derives from Dostoevsky and Camus.

A Note for Students

If you are new to studying Kelman, the 'classic' interviews with Duncan McLean and Kirsty McNeill are an excellent place to begin (see 'Further Reading'). Authorial intentions are not sacred, of course, but these interviews contain clear and often passionate explanations of Kelman's aims and agenda. The 2007 'Afterword' to *An Old Pub Near the Angel* is the best single source for those interested in Kelman's biography and formative literary influences. Cairns Craig's 'Resisting Arrest' is the seminal essay on Kelman's narrative technique.

I

Literary Forms

CHAPTER ONE

Early Kelman

Paul Shanks

James Kelman's importance as a writer lies in his successful and highly influential attempts to render working-class Glaswegian speech upon the page and his sharp awareness of literary form. His subtle understanding of voice and the implications of translating voice into text have led to a variety of experiments with language, narrative point of view and the representation of subjectivity. This chapter examines these features as they emerge in Kelman's early stories and first two novels, *The Busconductor Hines* and *A Chancer*, charting along the way some of the modernist preoccupations and literary influences which have shaped his writing.

Kelman began writing short stories in the late 1960s while living in London. By 1971 he had returned to his native Glasgow where he joined the Creative Writing Class at Glasgow University run by the extra-mural department. There he received encouragement and support from Philip Hobsbaum who was one of the first to recognise Kelman's talent.[1] Through Hobsbaum's then wife, American-born poet Anne Stevenson, he was introduced to the Texas-born short story writer, Mary Gray Hughes, and this contact eventually led to publication of *An Old Pub Near the Angel*. In an 'Afterword' to the 2007 reissue of this collection of stories, Kelman recalls that he 'had no experience of higher education and English Literature as a field of study but was used to discussing books and writers with various people in my various jobs since leaving school. [. . .] I read voraciously and wrote whenever possible.'[2] He was initially inspired by American writers such as Sherwood Anderson, Damon Runyon (and later Tillie Olsen), whose work approximated the rhythms of spoken language and whose subject matter concerned 'the lived-in, the everyday' (see Chapter 4).[3] At the same time, he was reading Dostoevsky, Gogol, Hamsun, Camus and, most notably, Kafka. For Kelman, these writers form an 'existential tradition in literature' that '[asserts] the primacy of the world as perceived and experienced by individual human beings' (see Chapter 11).[4] Through these influences Kelman gained a sense of the validity of his own culture and his own 'right to create art':

> I could sit down with my pen and paper and start doing stories of my own, from
> myself, the everyday trials and tribulations; my family, my boss, the boy and girl
> next door; the old guy telling yarns at the factory; whatever.[5]

The early stories published in *An Old Pub* have the brash and cocky exuber-
ance of a young writer learning his craft. As Kelman later remarked, 'the
author of *An Old Pub Near the Angel* is in his early twenties and with his
characters right at the heart of the experience; a smoke, a meal, sex, a beer,
the next bet, a relationship.'[6] These stories are notable for their dramatic
immediacy and have an upbeat quality when contrasted with the more pessimistic tone of later collections. Even in the story 'Abject Misery', where the
central character is penniless, hungry, cold and generally down on his luck,
we find defiant optimism:

> The rain started falling heavily.
> 'Who cares,' he shouted waving his fist upwards. 'Who cares anyway eh? My
> feet are soaking already ha ha ha.'[7]

More formally ambitious work is anticipated by 'The Cards' and 'An Old
Pub Near the Angel'. Here Kelman juxtaposes third-person narrative with
interior monologue in a way that propels the narrative forward while creating
effects of ambiguity and indeterminacy. In the title story, Charlie, following
an unexpected windfall of cash at the labour exchange, finds himself in an
empty pub with a half-deaf bartender for company. Toward the end of the
narrative, he encounters an old, possibly senile woman whose exclamations
he has difficulty understanding. His bafflement is complemented by the
rendering of the woman's speech on the page: 'goshtorafokelch'.[8] Here the
protagonist's perceptions are made concrete in the text, via a phonetically
represented series of sounds. As with much of Kelman's later work, such
effects point towards the narrative's orientation around a single point of view,
amid an overall sense of the uncanny. There are also examples of textual
play in the collection, a more pronounced feature of later work. Take, for
instance, the self-reflexive ending to 'The Cards': 'Jake picked out a book and
sat down to read.'[9] With this final sentence, the story concludes as the act of
reading begins.

An Old Pub is formally and thematically preoccupied with the difficulty
of communicating truth outside the perceptions of a single subject. In 'Nice
to be Nice', which centres upon a man whose main failing is that he is 'nice'
to the degree that others take advantage of him, the theme of miscommu-
nication is explored directly. The story, rendered in meticulous phonetic
Glaswegian, took Kelman several drafts to get right: 'Strange thing wis it
stertit oan a Wedinsday, A mean nothin ever sterts oan a Wedinsday kis

it's the day afore pay day in A'm ey skint. Mibby git a buckshee pint roon the Anchor, bit that's aboot it.'[10] Here speech sounds are replicated as they sound so, for instance, 'started' becomes 'stertit' and 'Wedinsday' gains a vowel to indicate the extra syllable. The text may at first present some difficulties to the reader. Even those familiar with Scots vernacular may find it hard, at first, to decipher unfamiliar written forms. However, this alienation effect is particularly apt for the narrator of 'Nice to be Nice' who, in his attempt to defend Moira, a single mother who is about to be evicted from her flat, is a man struggling to be heard. The final exclamation in the story is ironic in this respect, as it reveals both an underlying morality and an inability to effect that morality: 'a mean – nice tae be nice – know whit A mean?'[11] The story crystallises Kelman's approach to written narrative as a form of 'translation' or as an attempt to 'represent' the lives of those normally absent from mainstream fiction. The incomprehension of the reader – whether Glaswegian speech is 'native' or 'foreign' to him or her – complements the powerlessness of the central protagonist in his attempt to wrangle with forces threatening his immediate community.

Kelman later claimed that if he had known the phonetic poetry of Tom Leonard before writing 'Nice to be Nice', he would have approached the story quite differently.[12] Leonard's pared-down style and scrupulous rendering of utterance (and the pauses which define utterance) do filter into subsequent work. In *Three Glasgow Writers*, Kelman continues to develop a prose style informed by spoken Glaswegian both lexically and syntactically. However, the narrative voice has become more refined and aware of its limitations. This new approach is summed up by the 'Introductory' remarks preceding the collection:

I was born and bred in Glasgow
I have lived most of my life in Glasgow
It is the place I know best
My language is English
I write
In my writings the accent is in Glasgow
I am always from Glasgow and I speak English always
Always with this Glasgow accent

This is right enough[13]

Here, Kelman places emphasis on the locale from which his work originates and the language that is spoken there. The introduction also foregrounds a disjunction between speech and writing, and the difficulties which attend any effort to render speech accurately upon the page. In this sense, the final phrase, 'this is right enough', becomes both an affirmation (according to the familiar Glasgow/Scottish phrase) and an expression of linguistic uncertainty (as if to say, 'this is as right as it can be'). Taken as a whole, the introduction shows Kelman staking out the territory – linguistic, geographical and political – in which his best-known work operates.

The sense of difference, of a language which is both English and un-English, pervades nearly all of Kelman's first-person narratives collected in *Three Glasgow Writers*. In 'Remember Young Cecil', the vernacular is suggested through idiomatic phrase constructions ('I mind fine', 'in they days'); distinctively Scottish tense formations ('we all looks at one another'); and specific forms of colloquial language (the use of the term 'wide' to suggest someone 'street-wise').[14] In using these verbal signposts, Kelman manages to achieve a subtle, yet unemphatic, impression of Glasgow speech. This recognisably Glaswegian narrative voice forms an ideal framework for a story offering a brief glimpse into gambling subculture in Glasgow. In contrast to this vernacular idiom, however, certain phrases seem halting and oddly quantitative, as in the opening sentence of the story: 'Young Cecil is medium sized and retired.'[15]

If the narrative voice in 'Remember Young Cecil' suggests a community of people with shared values and aspirations, the voice of 'No Longer the Warehouseman' strikes a more solitary note. In this story, the 'speaker-narrator' is coming to terms with the fact he has just 'walked out' on a new job on the first day, after a long period on unemployment benefit.[16] He is evidently delaying the moment when he will have to go home and confront his wife with the information. A mock-bureaucratic, almost legalistic register is used to convey these facts. It is as though the speaker is setting out his problems in as abstract a manner as possible, in order to counteract their emotive weight: 'what matters is that I can no longer take gainful employment. That she understands does not mean I am acting correctly.'[17] However, the rhythms of spoken Glaswegian remain an implicit presence in this story and there are points at which the narrative voice suddenly switches into the vernacular, especially where it might amuse or shock the potential reader or listener:

> I am at a loss. At my age and considering my parental responsibilities, for example the wife and two weans, I should be paid more than twenty five pounds. I told the foreman this. It is a start he replied. Start fuck all I answered.[18]

The tension in the narrative derives from the formal register in which the character's private dilemmas are relayed. As in 'Nice to be Nice', Kelman suggests the political dimension to a personal crisis by exploring the language in which that crisis is articulated. The discrepancy between subject and idiom points towards an institutional discourse of upward mobility that falls short of material realities; the character's only source of strength lies in his ability to parody and subvert such discourses via his own thought-utterances (or 'inner-speech').[19]

Further experimentation with first-person monologue can be found in stories such as 'Jim Dandy', which concludes with a series of long unpunctuated phrases that serve to indicate the narrator's excitement and lack of control during a drunken seduction: 'she has moved her mouth forwards clinging along the tip with me there back lying out the game on the bed there and no not able to move at all knowing that door can open right now.'[20] In contrast, 'Where I was' adopts a form of present-tense interior monologue akin to the staccato utterances one might make into a recording device: 'A large dwelling house. It looks far from safe. [. . .] Apart from all this nothing of moment.'[21] The latter story, narrated by a man who has chosen a life on the open road after 'absconding' from his 'former abode', is the first of a sequence of thematically linked 'itinerant' stories which Kelman wrote in the 1970s and early 1980s. All of these were subsequently published in the collection Lean Tales (also featuring the work of Alasdair Gray and Agnes Owens). In these stories, nameless narrators recount fragmentary episodes from wandering life in various locations in Scotland, Wales, the Channel Islands and London. The narratives are often fragmentary, episodic and inconclusive.[22] Prosaic features of the natural world induce brief, mysterious epiphanies, ranging from a moment of blankness while sheltering by a loch ('Where I was') to the discovery of red sandworms after a stormy night spent in a beach shelter ('Getting there') or the erratic movements of a colony of ants in a dishevelled patch of grass ('the same is here again'). The stories are predominantly set outside of Glasgow, but the Glasgow accent through which they are recounted provides a firm sense of the speakers' regional and class origins.

The narrative idiom of the 'itinerant tales' bears uncanny similarities with Samuel Beckett's post-war fiction. A recurring preoccupation with the body and its excesses, especially those pertaining to the feet, groin and arse, recalls Beckett narrators who often linger upon their physical dysfunctions. (The narrator of the novellas speaks of his childhood incontinence, adult constipation and painful feet, while in the later Trilogy there is enough cursing of testicles, aching cracks and bodily excretions, not to mention weak kidneys and shrinking limbs, to fill a literary sanatorium.) The instances of bodily decrepitude in Kelman's stories are perhaps more pragmatically realised, more realistically evoked, than those which abound in the Trilogy. However, the overall effect can be uncannily similar, especially in 'the same is here again' where the narrator refers to his poor teeth, aching 'chopper', stinking feet and facial pustules with the ironic and self-effacing humour, the use of negation and self-parody, that is so recognisable a feature of Beckett's writing.[23] A propensity for excessive systematisation also resonates; while there are no examples in Kelman's work that quite reach the length of the sucking stones episode in *Molloy* (where the narrator explains, for several pages, his habit of distributing and alternating sucking stones), Kelman's characters also attempt to cope with their material shortcomings through methodical strictness:

> Up until the wash I was wearing each pair of socks on alternate days, I wore both when sleeping. They had a stale, damp smell. My feet were never wholly dry. Small particles stuck to the toejoints, the soles of the feet. I had to see it all everyday when I made the change of socks. In future I shall steel myself if it means warmer feet. And may even take to wearing both pairs daily, in other words keep them on at all times.[24]

This extract also displays the propensity for narrative negation and self-correction which characterises the itinerant tales as a whole. Kelman describes this narrative style in some detail in the essay 'Artists and Value'. He defines the technique as 'negative apprehension' or 'the subjunctive mood' and sees it as typical of Franz Kafka: 'what [Kafka] often does is refer to a space which he then fills with a crowd of things that either don't exist, or maybe don't exist. He fills the page with absences and possible absences, possible realities.'[25]

Kelman certainly draws upon Kafka in experimenting with narrative doubt and negation, although it is perhaps in Beckett's work that the technique reaches its apotheosis. We can see Kelman beginning to adopt this method of composition in *Three Glasgow Writers* and other early stories; in 'Not not while the giro', the technique becomes structurally intrinsic. The title itself with its use of a double negative, a semantic 'knot', becomes a formula for the entrapment of many Kelman protagonists. The story concerns a man in his thirties, a self-professed 'neerdowell' with a 'deathwish', engaged in inner dialogue as his material circumstances appear more and more hopeless.[26] Not much of note transpires over the course of the narrative. The narrator smokes the last of his tobacco, babysits for his landlady, signs on at the local 'broo', engages in sexual fantasies, contemplates suicide and plans to become a traveller of Scotland's coasts. The basis of the drama is entirely within the narrator's embittered consciousness in which a ceaseless and seemingly self-perpetuating dialogue takes place:

> The current me is my heart's desire. Surely not. Yet it appears the case. I am always needing money and I am always getting rid of it. [. . .] Not even a question of wrecking my life, just that I am content to wallow. Nay enjoy. I should commit suicide.[27]

A further dimension to the character's predicament in 'Not not while the giro' is suggested via the framework of the narrative. The story opens, seemingly randomly, in mid-sentence and concludes without a recognisable full stop, as if the inner speech of the character has been caught with all the arbitrariness of a tape machine. The use of block paragraphs (as well as foregrounding interrupted and unfinished thoughts) further connotes the mechanistic dimension to the narrative, intimating not only the silences that lie between the characters' interior thoughts but the 'recorded' nature of the text, presented as though mentally overheard. This quality is emphasised in a more expansive way in novels like *A Chancer* and *The Busconductor Hines*. In this sense, Kelman's writing grapples with not only the immediate crises of his characters but also the *structure* of their experience.

Perhaps Kafka's thought-provoking series of prose sketches, *Meditations*, formed the inspiration for Kelman's third collection of stories, *Short Tales from the Nightshift* (1978). In this pamphlet (published at the Third Eye Centre), Kelman chose a shorter and more cryptic narrative mode than in earlier work. The booklet includes anecdotal pieces (such as 'Manufactured in Paris' and 'Busted Scotch'), urban myths ('The Habits of Rats' and 'Acid') and prose meditations ('The Place' and 'An Enquiry Concerning Human Understanding'). Many of these were republished in subsequent collections but it is pertinent to note Kelman's exclusive focus on the form at this stage in his writing. In interview, Kelman has claimed that his decision to write these shorter pieces was initiated by economic necessity in that he was raising a family and working full time. In short, he did not have the space or time in which to write more extended narratives.[28]

The most significant of these *Short Tales* (in so far as it has reappeared not only in *Lean Tales* but also in the *Collected Stories*) is 'Learning the Story', a self-reflexive piece of writing which hints at both the voyeuristic aspects of storytelling and the insufficiencies of narrative as a means of representing the 'other'. In the opening two sentences, we are offered a simple synopsis or summary of the 'story': 'I once met an old lady sitting under a bridge over the River Kelvin. She smoked Capstan full-strength cigarettes and played the mouthorgan.'[29] In the second paragraph, these details are enlarged into a dramatic set-piece which is rendered in a melodramatic, almost archaic, style: 'Aye, she cried again. And rising to her feet she brought out the mouthorgan from somewhere inside the layers of her clothing, and struck up the tune: Maxwelton Braes Are Bonny.'[30] The reference to the ballad, 'Annie Laurie', adds to the sense of nostalgia and the uncanny. However, in the final paragraph, the narrative switches in tone once again:

The old lady wore specs and had a scarf wrapped round her neck. Her nose was bony. Her skirt may have showed under the hem of her coat. When she was playing the mouthorgan she had moved slightly from foot to foot. Her coat was furry.[31]

With this transition, the narrative attains the tonality of Kafka's fiction (especially shorter narratives such as 'On the Tram' and 'Absent-minded Window-gazing'). The scrupulous way in which the details of the woman's outward appearance are itemised is legalistic (although the idiom, in this instance, is not), as if the speaker were hunting for substantive evidence. However, the narrator's arbitrary choice of which features to isolate creates an overall sense of fragmentation and provisionality. In this sense, the final observation on the 'furriness' of the woman's coat is humorously subjective. Ultimately, the more details we are given concerning the woman, the less is revealed; the more the speaker 'learns' the story, the more it gets bogged down in circumstantial details, and the less it becomes a story. (This style is reminiscent of the novels of Alain Robbe-Grillet.) A similar effect can be found in 'Sarah Crosbie', a tale constructed from tendentious and inconclusive information but which hints at happenings of a criminal or supernatural nature. The reader, like the reporter who ends up visiting Sarah Crosbie, may try to fill in the gaps but this will yield no certainties.[32]

In interview, Kelman has claimed that his shorter works, as well as a way of utilising limited time, became a way of flexing his literary muscles.[33] Certainly, the shorts published later in *Greyhound for Breakfast* have a playful and occasionally surreal quality while also exploring, as with 'Learning the Story', problems of perspective and narrative point of view. Kelman has stated that it was via these prose experiments that he gained the confidence to attempt his most formally ambitious novel, *Translated Accounts*.[34] However, it was while creating these succinct and sometimes opaque sketches in the 1970s that Kelman was working on two more substantial projects.

It is important to note the close relationship between *The Busconductor Hines* and *A Chancer* as the form of one text is often illuminated through a reading of the other. It was while working on both of these novels that Kelman found the narrative objectivity that he was striving towards.[35] For much of *A Chancer*, Kelman adopts an external perspective, whereas in *Hines* the interior thoughts of the main protagonist are framed within a seemingly objective authorial framework. In *Hines*, Kelman found a method of entering the consciousness of his protagonist without creating a scission between narrative voice and character and without losing the objectivity of a third-person narrative point of view (a form of free indirect discourse mixed with interior monologue). In the following exchange, a relatively neutral narrative voice switches, almost imperceptibly, into the voice of Rab Hines:

> Paul rose from the floor with his thumb still in his mouth, his gaze shifting a moment to capture the tin; and he was passing it to Hines without any sign of resentment; just a thing to be done, you pass tobacco tins to the auld man.[36]

The challenge in *A Chancer*, by contrast, was to hint at consciousness entirely in terms of outward signs. One of the many effects achieved through this narrative style is to create a sense of horror through understatement. In one such episode, Tammas begins work at a copper factory where he is required to help operate a machine that creates copper wires. The almost acrobatic finesse required in order to learn the skills requisite for the job and the nature of the rolling machine itself are described in functional language. The almost filmic fly-on-the wall perspective adopted in *A Chancer* is further accentuated by gaps in the text which come to suggest moments of blankness or, according to Cairns Craig, those points at which being is suspended.[37] Take, for instance, the episode in which Tammas walks to Scotstoun in order to pay his friend Rab a visit. Over the course of his journey, he passes disused factories and gap-sites, and passes through pedestrian tunnels all described in seemingly monochrome colours. Throughout, these details manage to create an accumulating sense of the uncanny which reaches crescendo when Tammas pauses at a pedestrian tunnel which passes beneath the river: 'the floor was white with bird shit. Condensation seeped down the walls and roofing and there was a continuous gurgling noise coming from somewhere, also a roaring noise that increased the further downstairs he stepped, until it seemed to block out all other sound'.[38] At this point, the narrative breaks off and resumes when Tammas is 'on the other side of the river', suggesting a moment of blankness and absence.[39]

The formal experimentation of these novels complements their underlying politics. The present-tense consciousness of Hines recalls the interior monologues of Joyce in more than a stylistic sense. Rab Hines, like Stephen Dedalus (and, to a lesser extent, Leopold Bloom) in *Ulysses*, is highly self-conscious of his internal dialogues, and the rhetoric that he adopts is often distinguished by its performative quality. As with Joyce, the textual rendering of inner thought points towards an alienation that impinges upon the relationship between public and private space. The protagonist of *The Busconductor Hines* has a self-conscious awareness (sometimes verging on 'the paranoiac', to deploy a key Kelman term) of the mediated nature of his internal thought-utterances.[40] In this sense the reader not only appears to overhear Rab Hines as he engages in inner dialogue; the character also overhears himself. Because Kelman has dissolved the hierarchy separating speech from narration, the boundaries between public utterance and private thought become tenuous to the extent that it sometimes becomes difficult to determine whether the character is speaking aloud or giving voice to his thoughts inwardly. An Irish-Scottish cultural perspective becomes a cogent means of assessing this mode of representing consciousness. For the characters who people Joyce's Dublin and Kelman's Glaswegian protagonists alike, there is an awareness of being culturally subordinate and framed within a hierarchy

of power which infiltrates subjectivity itself. The psychological and historical consequences of this mode of existence are epitomised in *Ulysses* when
Stephen Dedalus claims that 'the cracked lookingglass of a servant' is an apt
'symbol of Irish art'.[41] For Rab Hines, inner alienation stems from the ways
in which he has come to view himself as 'other': 'had a mirror been handy he
could have watched his face. It would have been interesting to witness the
outward appearance.'[42] The politics that underlie these instances of inner and
outer dislocation are heightened and more explicitly stated in Kelman's later
novels (especially *A Disaffection*).

Unlike Hines, Tammas frequently *chooses* not to articulate his thoughts
and thereby manages to avoid the suffocating spiral of interiority which
Kelman's other protagonists endure. Tammas is a man of actions, not
words; he tends not to analyse or comment on his behaviour and resents
it when family and friends coerce him into 'explaining himself'. At one
point, Auld Phil, who works at the bookies, gives Tammas the following
advice: 'you're best to say nothing. Never tell a soul. Nothing. The best
way.'[43] This statement becomes a signature for a way of life and Tammas's
various evasive strategies. The ethos of 'giving nothing away' and of 'saying
nothing' suggests deliberate subterfuge rather than existential blankness
and the author is complicit with this strategy in that he chooses to add to
the silence rather than to talk over his character: to *show* rather than to
tell.

The overall form and arrangement of *A Chancer* and *Hines* serve to enact
key themes. One notable feature of the latter novel is the running visual
motif which subdivides the text; this might be described as a series of hollow
ellipses or bullet points. The ellipsis appears to alter in meaning throughout
the text. Its first appearance seems indicative of a familiar self-reflexive (post)
modernist trope:

> [...] settling back on his chair he opened the book.
>
> o o o [44]

The visual interruption to the narrative draws attention to the act of reading
(thereby recalling the conclusion to 'The Cards'), yet its appearance is also
the first indication of a sense of absence or emptiness which pervades the
novel. The ellipsis also becomes an emphatic punctuation mark, indicating
the gaps between Hines's life at home and the relationship which he holds
with his workmates at the bus depot. The ellipsis continues to shift in meaning
throughout the text; on a typographical level it comes to represent a clock-in
sign, a bus queue or a 'trio of pots'.[45] In the wider scheme of the novel, it refers
to the family unit of three and to Hines's third term at bus-conducting; on yet

another level, it indicates the controlled and structured time, the 'clockwork universe', which dominates Hines's life.[46]

In *A Chancer*, ellipses are used in a similar manner (although this time they are solid rather than hollow). Much of the novel is structured around recurring patterns of silence and absence, and these are formally represented on the page through the use of blank space and ellipses which divide the text. The ellipses gradually come to emphasise both the inarticulacy and wilful subterfuge of Tammas, a young working-class Glaswegian who becomes increasingly caught up in the gambling world and lifestyle. The economic and cultural bases of these silences are hinted at through the gaps in the text; they comment upon a mode of existence where individual autonomy is crushed by a paralysing awareness of economic and personal restriction. However, as the novel progresses, these ellipses also attain a more positive definition, coming to represent the energy that drives Tammas from one betting episode to the next.

This chapter has considered what I take to be the most significant stylistic and thematic developments in Kelman's early novels and short stories. His ability to create ambiguity and indeterminacy via narrative idiom and point of view, his capacity in rendering the voice of an indigenous culture on the page while illustrating the difficulties and limitations of such an endeavour, are all self-evident in these texts. What also comes to the fore is Kelman's preoccupation with the private crises of his protagonists and their public expression; this key concern is further explored in his subsequent works.

CHAPTER TWO

How late it was, how late and Literary Value

Mary McGlynn

Much to his own dismay, James Kelman is best known to the general public for one of the most contentious literary awards of recent times. In 1994 he received Britain's most prestigious literary award, the Booker Prize, despite the objections of several of the judging committee's members, including Rabbi Julia Neuberger, who publicly denounced Kelman's victory.[1] The controversy surrounding the winning book, *How late it was, how late*, was on its surface about 'profanity' and the novel's lower-class, quasi-indigent protagonist. Above all, it was about the word 'fuck'. To critics its mere frequency (one tabloid newspaper estimated 4,000 instances) proved the novel's baseness. Kelman countered by insisting 'my culture and my language have the right to exist,'[2] and objected that debating the propriety of 'swear words' in literature 'beg[s] the question of what those words are [. . .] involving me again in a value system that *isn't your own to deny*'.[3] This concern with a seemingly lowbrow feature has roots in highbrow technical detail; stretches of *How late* contain no so-called profanity at all (notably, the final three pages) while variations on the word 'fuck' occur twenty-four times on page 57 alone. The uneven distribution of this powerful yet everyday word suggests meticulous formal patterning and hints at the inadequacy of simplistic approaches to the novel and the cultural debates surrounding it. To grasp why *How late* touched such a nerve, we must move beyond mere counting – tallying the swear words, insults, and accolades – to examine the systems of exchange and valuation the novel participates in, willingly and otherwise.

The row over Kelman's Booker victory is but one instalment in his encounters with the prize committee. Although his third novel, *A Disaffection*, was shortlisted in 1989, Kelman did not attend the award ceremony. Reportedly, 'he had better things to do than swan around with the literati' and instead spent the day tutoring in Glasgow, a choice consistent with his view that 'the London literary establishment is not a good thing for literature.'[4] Given that a judge had declared Kelman's 1984 submission *The Busconductor Hines* one of the two worst novels under consideration that year, describing it incredulously (and inaccurately) as 'written entirely in Glaswegian!', it seems likely

Kelman did not expect to win in 1989, and he was not present when Kazuo Ishiguro's *The Remains of the Day* took the award. That novel's strong sales and subsequent adaptation into an Oscar-nominated film show the Booker Prize at its commercially and culturally most powerful. Ishiguro's novel regularly appears on reading lists for student exams in English-speaking countries around the world and continues to sell tens of thousands of copies annually. Kelman's two shortlisted novels, conversely, and despite strong critical reception, declare themselves distinctly Scottish rather than British, working-class rather than genteel, and long and difficult rather than short and accessible; neither has come near lifetime sales by Ishiguro's winner. (Figures from Chris Fowler, subject librarian at the Booker archive, suggest *How late* to be selling at about half the rate of *Remains*, with *A Disaffection* substantially behind both.) Kelman's decision to sit out the 1989 Booker ceremony might be seen as a refusal of the very notion of the literary award (as, perhaps, involving him in a value system he rejects), but his willingness in 1994 to attend and accept the prize shows a cannier balancing of artistic principle and commercial interest.

The Booker Prize enacts a similar balancing of aesthetic and economic value. In many respects, books are saleable commodities like any others produced and consumed via the conventional industrial channels. Materialist (Marxist) thought calls the price such commodities fetch on the marketplace their 'exchange value'; attention from the Booker Prize committee is effectively free marketing for publishers, and almost always translates into increased demand for their product and, ultimately, higher sales and profits. Commodities also, however, have 'use value' – intrinsic worth based on their own characteristics and utility, irrespective of supply and demand. A book may not generate wealth for its creator, but still possess profound aesthetic value; John Milton sold *Paradise Lost* to his printer for £5. 'Use value' is qualitative, and much less easy to determine than exchange value – especially in the case of artworks, whose intrinsic qualities are so intangible, and whose 'worth' is historically variable. The role of the literary prize is complex here, effectively *investing* the work with the value it supposedly 'measures' as an intrinsic feature of the work; the imprimatur of a Booker Prize victory practically guarantees lasting 'literary' status. This endows the prizes themselves with great power. The activity of perceiving/conferring elusive 'literary' qualities in a novel – distinguishing works of genuine and enduring aesthetic worth from mediocre books which may sell more copies – this process itself reinforces the values of the people and institutions doing the classifying. Tasteful judges thus derive status from the cultural value their decision attributes to the artwork. The French sociologist Pierre Bourdieu calls this function of taste 'cultural capital', drawing on materialist terms where capital refers to accumulated goods that can be used to produce other goods. Cultural capital encompasses all the resources – accumulated knowledge, habits, values and ideas – we use to 'produce' the social status we inhabit, whether 'cultured', discriminating and urbane, or popular, unpretentious and accessible. The 'credibility' of an authoritative judge comprises the values we wish to see affirmed. 'Appreciating' art functions as both *evidence* and *exercise* of 'good taste' on these terms.

Bourdieu contends that how and why tastes are formed is ultimately a reflection of social hierarchy ('taste classifies, and it classifies the classifier'[5]). A host of critics have developed this line of inquiry. Barbara Herrnstein Smith argues that literary value is always constructed rather than absolute, that objective aesthetic criteria to evaluate works of art do not exist, yet neither are such criteria entirely subjective. Evaluation is a social practice, albeit dominated by cultural elites. John Guillory emphasises that there have always been parallel processes of assigning worth, one on aesthetic merit and the other on economic viability. Drawing from Guillory's work, John Frow emphasises the *incommensurability* of these two 'evaluative regimes' – the impossibility of aligning or reconciling their criteria.

The Booker Prize's history and press coverage bear witness to these tensions, but spill beyond the cultural sphere and into the 'real' economy. The origins of the prize lie in the world of transnational capitalism as the Booker company, a large food wholesaler, 'sought to address the shift from an imperial to a post-imperial reality.'[6] Reducing its colonial holdings in Guyana, what was then known as Booker-McConnell purchased copyrights of well-known English writers and soon after agreed to sponsor a literary prize. When the corporation became a benefactor of the arts, it participated in a longstanding exchange between those with cultural capital and those with financial capital in which the latter appropriates the right to judge the former, a process Bourdieu calls 'consecration'. As Graham Huggan sees it, such a cultural prize brings authors, publishers, booksellers, critics, the media and judges

> into productive interaction; it also brings into relief the continuing evaluative process by which the literary text is constructed as an object of negotiation between different interest groups [. . .] The prize literalizes the principle of evaluative investment by drawing attention to the consecrating role played by the financial sponsor.[7]

The central role of money should be clear here – the 'investment' of literary value in the winning novel by the prize is ultimately derived from the sponsor's financial endowment, and it produces real economic returns for publishers. No matter how often participants in the judging process cite literary criteria, even those with differing aesthetic agendas have a financial stake in there being as much publicity as possible. James English notes that even the

predictable critiques of the Booker, and the nearly annual scandals surrounding it, serve to strengthen its prestige and increase the visibility of players on
the cultural stage. Precisely through decrying the impact of the commercial
world on the literary one, artists, critics and the public reinforce the illusion
of their separation.[8]

More than in most years, the (actively manufactured) drama of the judging
in the year of Kelman's Booker victory unearthed contradictions binding
together the various participants in the faux scandals. The 1994 competition
raised eyebrows long before the result was announced. Judge James Wood
advocated for a book on the longlist (the competition reduced 130 nominees
to five finalists) without revealing himself to be married to its author, one
shortlisted book had been privately published after fourteen presses rejected
it, and another novel on the shortlist contained homosexual themes and
explicit sex. A backdrop to these blips of controversy was the widespread
impression that the 'boring' list was failing to generate large sales, certainly
nothing like the 320,000 copies sold of the previous year's winner, Roddy
Doyle's Paddy Clarke Ha ha ha.[9] The expectation that shortlisting will lead
to a 'Booker boost' in sales is part of the carefully managed contradiction of
the prize system; while the prize's own longtime spokesman, Martyn Goff,
asserts that the award purports to seek 'the best book of the year, regardless
of publicity or whether it will sell', the same Booker public relations machine
predicts that an author's sales will increase 'fivefold' with a victory.[10] As
Nicola Pitchford remarks,

> from the beginning, the Booker Prize [. . .] has embodied fundamental cultural
> and national contradictions. It was designed as both a publicity venture aimed
> at the general public and as a shot in the arm for elite, 'serious' literature.
> [. . .] [The Prize administrators] have worked to cultivate a sense of popular
> enfranchisement.[11]

How late might seem well suited to bridge the distance between the popular
and the literary. While Kelman is often compared to Samuel Beckett and
has the media profile of a serious literary novelist, his protagonist, Sammy
Samuels, is uneducated, unlucky and uncouth, a far cry from the refined
world of the London publishing scene. In the wake of Paddy Clarke's victory,
bookmakers anticipated victory for another expletive-laced working-class
story. (The fact that odds are placed on the shortlist contenders lends the
appearance of popular, even working-class, appeal to the annual Booker spectacle, though Pitchford convincingly demonstrates that the presence of the
Booker odds in high-street betting shops is paid-for promotional activity.[12])
Conservative newspapers bemoaned the 'corruption' of the English language
and lack of identifiable plot in the novel, and reports in the weeks prior to the

decision gave anecdotal evidence of low sales. But ultimately, after tense and complex deliberations, three of the five judges cast votes for a Kelman win.[13]

Following the award ceremony, however, Rabbi Neuberger voiced her vehement dismay, labelling *How late* as 'crap', an ironically profane comment to make about a book she disliked partially for its own crass language.[14] The subsequent weeks saw Kelman and his defenders asserting his right to use whatever language he chose, while detractors pointed to ongoing poor sales figures as evidence of the novel's unworthiness. The Booker Prize and its aftermath thus framed discussion about Kelman's novel in economic and sociological terms, treating the novel as a test of the relationship of cultural capital and marketability. Both sides of this debate saw the text as offering authentic insight into a certain type or social class, a tendency which ignored the novel's formal innovations and artistry, exactly the regime of value a Booker Prize is supposed to reward.

Kelman says he regrets his victory, particularly its ongoing commercial effect:

> The hostility, the attacks interfered with my work such in a way that I don't think ever really recovered. [*sic*] [. . .] When you have bookshops saying, 'we won't stock this guy's books', it makes it difficult for the people who sell you [. . .] affects the budget set aside to promote your work. It's an economic decision.[15]

Contradicting English's argument that scandal benefits all the actors in prize dramas, Kelman suggests this method of accumulating and bestowing value has not profited him or his books. His reference to both his artistic efforts and their economic context is illuminating, indicating that he does not hold an idealistic view of art as unconnected to the marketplace. And indeed, the idea that art could have such independence is in keeping with the conventional notions of literary value that Kelman explicitly rejects. In noting that literary judgements have negative financial consequences for a working writer, Kelman asserts a link between the two that parallels moves he makes in his fiction but which is often obscured by scholarly and critical agendas.

If Kelman's reputation suffered in the popular sphere, it has been consistently positive amongst scholars. In the wake of the Booker controversy, a number of scholarly studies appeared which approvingly linked Kelman's style to that of high modernists, his themes to existentialists, and his allusions to any number of works of the Western canon, books deemed high in cultural capital. While Kelman's ready engagement with such texts is evident in all his novels, not least *A Disaffection* and *How late*, he is well aware that critics regularly make assumptions about both his knowledge and that of his characters. In a 1989 interview, Kelman observes that the protagonist of

The Busconductor Hines is someone who has read Dostoevsky and Camus, but 'because the central character works at an ordinary, so-called unskilled, labouring job, very few contemporary critics ever conceive that [the story] could be of formal interest to them'.[16] Kelman points out here not just stereotypes about working-class reading habits but also the prevalent expectation that fiction about the working class will be formally conservative; that is, working-class fiction is presumed to be realist, not experimental. So while scholars are more than willing to accept the literary value of Kelman's œuvre, he feels they do so in part by conforming his works to their own pre-existing value system rather than noting his challenges to such systems.

Most reviewers praised Kelman's next novel, *A Disaffection*, acknowledging the author's mastery of his language and his deft deployment of literary and philosophical intertexts. Martin Kirby, however, saw the life of a disenchanted Scottish schoolteacher as over-explored terrain, suggesting Kelman write about a Scottish burglar instead. Of course, *How late* did, ironically, focus on a thief and ex-convict; no doubt Kirby's suggestion of protagonist for a sequel was shaped by his knowledge of Kelman's own background, the commentary thus serving to firm up boundaries of both genre and class. Kirby also found fault with *A Disaffection*'s stream-of-consciousness style, its intense focus on the wild and desperate inner life of Patrick Doyle, saying it provided 'not very much dramatic excitement'.[17] Drawing on similar stereotypes, Jill Neville's approving review remarks that 'at one point Patrick's unemployed brother and his cronies enjoy a mammoth drinking bout. [. . .] an important bonding ritual.'[18] Her choice of the anthropological term 'ritual', as well as the omission of Patrick himself from the list of drinkers, reveal a class-induced bias that exonerates the schoolteacher protagonist. Both critiques are representative of middle-class/mainstream expectations that more 'exotic' characters be rendered in a more conventional narrative style, something Kelman identifies as 'the usual elitism'.[19]

But when reviewers accept Patrick Doyle as 'one of us' because of his education and recognisable angst, they paper over how partial and provisional his class allegiances are, overlooking precisely the qualities in this novel that will open Kelman's next to such critique, like the consumption of alcohol and the use of profanity. In praising the local vernacular, the innovative narrative voice and paranoia about state institutions, they laud what will be condemned in *How late*. Should theorists of value like Frow, Smith and Bourdieu seek evidence of the role context plays in aesthetic evaluation, the discussion by reviewers of Patrick's supposed middle-class status and Sammy's working-class one certainly affirms a double standard.

Further evidence of a double standard can be found in attitudes toward the characters' drinking habits. Tellingly, reviewers of *A Disaffection* tend not to dwell on the drinking habits of its white-collar protagonist. We do frequently observe Patrick under the influence of alcohol, his relationship with drink noticeably problematic even in a milieu where it is a Friday tradition for schoolteachers to hit the bar 'for a couple of jars' at lunch.[20] Yet the shield of job, education and allusive musings seems to exempt Patrick from reproach, while critical censure of Sammy reveals preconceptions about working-class characters that interfere with plot-level comprehension. With such review titles as 'In Holy Boozers' and 'Glaswegian gets Booker with tale of blind drunk', critics reflect the popular perception of the heavy-drinking Scottish working class; writing in *The Times*, Simon Jenkins goes even further, linking form to content via a comparison of reading the novel to being berated by a drunken, profanity-spewing Glaswegian.[21] Yet *How late* never depicts Sammy inebriated. When he ventures into the bar where Helen works and then on to his own local, he remains parsimonious, drinking in sum two pints and two whiskies. He has one beer, unfinished, in the final moments of the novel, making a total of five drinks in ten days. This is not to say that Sammy did not drink to excess in his lost weekend but rather to point out that one bender is too easily extrapolated to be a chronic condition, a personality failing, and a damning trait of an entire class. More tellingly, the prose style dismissively misread as a consequence of the character's intoxicated state is actually a painstaking stylistic choice of Kelman's.

Just as Sammy's drinking is misapprehended, so are his culture and language. While the educated reading public seems to link absence of cash and presence of intoxication, the equation Kelman sets forth is an opposite one. Sammy's lack of money excludes him from the pub culture that can be taken as the basis of his social network, laying bare his friendlessness and suggesting that, contrary to romanticisations of working-class culture, it is just as imbricated in capitalist systems of exchange as the lifestyles of the more affluent. Without the ability to buy drinks for those he meets, Sammy does not feel entitled to enter a pub – while he briefly contemplates 'touching' a mate or bartender for a loan, his cultural habits resist such a practice.

Cultural norms are very much in play. Kelman's pyrotechnic profanity challenges marginalisation of certain words and displays an art form that has been regularly and strategically devalued. Sammy delights in his language and in its effect on others. He amuses himself in elaborations and inventions: 'Fuck it but he was tired, he was just bloody tired; knackered and drained, knackered and drained; nay energy; nay fuck all; he just wanted to sleep, to sleep and then wake up; refreshed and fucking enerfuckinggetic, enerfuckinggenetised.'[22] 'Fuck' functions here as multiple parts of speech, and its ability to fulfil multiple grammatical functions belies the notion that Sammy lacks expressivity. Rather, his rhythmic riff on exhaustion reveals that he recognises language as a tool he can play with.

Not that 'fuck' is always a joyful word. At one point during his second imprisonment, Sammy reflects that he would struggle as much to get home this time as the last, 'cause he had nay stick and he had nay fucking dough man he was skint, fuckt, the usual'.[23] The accumulation of synonyms under-lines his condition and shows his anxiety; money itself is the trigger for the use of the word 'fuck' as well as itself synonymous with absence. Profanity functions as a stand-in for economic critique; its rejection by both sympa-thetic and antagonistic readers speaks to their distance from such economi-cally straitened circumstances, a reflexive devaluing of certain people and their language. Dougal McNeill is right to point out that Kelman 'insists on a class language', but in arguing that *How late* 'is a narrative of inexpressive and caged un-expressiveness' relying on profanity to 'underline its tensions and limits', he overlooks how carefully Kelman orchestrates his expletives.[24] It is commonplace to suggest that swearing, especially in its repetition, is an indication of poverty of idea or vocabulary, but the uncritical acceptance of the premise would seem part of a mindset of 'generous but misdirected roman-ticism' much like Patrick's.[25] Kelman's efforts to resist the assigning of value to specific words is in keeping with his larger project of pointing out that art belongs to all classes and that hierarchies are imposed, not innate.

The disproportionate critical attention to what Kelman has derisively called 'the sweary words' segregates them from other stylised linguistic choices he makes.[26] Examining them in connection with other formal devices allows us better to see how Kelman's language participates in and comments on systems of valuation. As Liam McIlvanney so succinctly puts it, 'expletives, hesitation, repetition, aposiopesis [deliberate incompletion of a phrase for dra-matic effect]: much of the dynamism of Kelman's prose derives from elements of communication which have no definable semantic content.'[27] McIlvanney suggests here that open-ended sentences, repetitive prose, and words like 'fuck' and 'em' convey meaning via context, not their definitions; he goes on to argue that it is Kelman's disinclination to describe or speak for his characters that motivates this choice. But this analysis can privilege the mimetic ability of language. If instead the link among these devices is that they usually lack linguistic *value*, Kelman escapes the burden of representation. In using these techniques, he seeks less to represent realistic speech patterns than to recuper-ate linguistic forms that have themselves been marginalised. The effect is to reject the existing system of value, moving emphasis from *what* is said to *how* it is said, so we do not just hear Sammy's story but assimilate his voice.

While Sammy is in the bath he anticipates for the first third of the novel, he suddenly feels that he is not alone. Realising that the front door is unlocked, he starts to worry:

> that fucking door outside man he hadnay fucking snibbed it for fuck sake he hadnay even fucking snibbed it! imagine no even snibbing the fucking thing! fucking idiot man, fuck sake, crazy fucking

Okay.
He breathed in through his nose, relaxed the shoulders.[28]

In addition to the repetition, expletives, and aposiopesis, we see other
Kelman trademarks that represent supposed linguistic poverty – cliché, non-
standard English, absence of capital letters, excessive punctuation, missing
punctuation. What's important here is not how convincingly Sammy's panic
is evoked; attention to such 'realism' leaves intact a linguistic hierarchy in
which these words are empty of meaning. Rather, what is significant is the
insistence that meaning *is* conveyed. As Sammy struggles to calm down,
he relaxes his shoulders, but even as the narrative voice leaves the agitated
mental state, it retains Sammy's locution – 'the' shoulders. Neuberger explicitly charged that *How late* 'never changes in tone'.[29] While the narrator does
reveal supple command of a variety of registers, at this moment at least,
Neuberger is right; we do not leave Sammy's language, which makes it the
language of story and interpretation, not just having value but determining
value.

In order to establish what constitutes 'value' for Sammy, let us turn to the
ways money is discussed and the actual amounts exchanged in the course of
the roughly twelve days *How late* spans. Beginning on a Sunday morning, the
text shows Sammy coming to consciousness in a vacant lot, hung over and
broke, wearing another man's trainers. We learn about Sammy's financial
situation anterior to the novel mainly through his flashbacks to the final
argument he had with his girlfriend Helen before he left the council flat she
rents and he shares with her. During this final row with Helen we learn that
Sammy is on the dole, working only sporadically as an unskilled manual
labourer on construction sites and otherwise supplementing his income by
'earning' – shoplifting and then reselling clothing like dress shirts and leather
jackets. After leaving the flat on the Friday, Sammy seems to have gone on
a two-day drinking binge in which he 'blagged' a jacket, used the proceeds
to bet on some horses, won big (£120), and spent all he accumulated.[30] The
terminology here redefines economic activity so that stealing is part of the
exchange economy; at the same time, it is noteworthy that Sammy functions
almost entirely outside of the official labour market.

When Sammy calls himself 'skint', he does not speak in the rough meta-
phorical terms that we tend to use in discussing finances. Rather, for the first
portion of the novel, for six days, Sammy is entirely, irredeemably broke. He
awakens with no money in his pockets and, on the Wednesday, his first foray
into the outside world after his beating by the police and ensuing blindness
is complicated by the fact that he lacks the bus fare to get home. He eats
only what is already in the kitchen, not engaging in any financial transac-
tions until his giro money arrives on Friday morning. Even then, Sammy is

frugal, responsible, careful, spending only on foodstuffs, a pair of sunglasses, and public transport to various government offices. Gustav Klaus character-ises 'skint' as experiential, provisional, and reflecting a 'genuine' proletarian relationship to money:

> Being skint is a transient state [. . .] this alternation between being 'skint' and having cash [. . .] defines their situation, an eternal up and down, without issue or progress. Money, when available, is there to be spent: on smoke, drink and grub. But its possession carries little value in itself; for most of these characters it is emphatically not a means of buying status, security, a home or family.[31]

Money itself has only exchange value for Klaus's working class, with the implication that it has other meanings for those who can accumulate it. Kelman's discontent with his Booker seems analogous; its exchange value has meaning to him, while its cultural purchase does not. In rejecting the cultural value bestowed, Kelman stands alongside his devalued characters.

Even the word 'sightloss', repeatedly used by the bureaucrats and state employees in *How late*, reinforces Sammy's devaluing by society. A Kelman coinage that sounds at once technical and noncommittal, it implies judge-ment, as 'loss' suggests fault or neglect. Indeed, most of Sammy's interlocutors either doubt his blindness or question its source, deploying the rhetoric of responsibility to assert Sammy's accountability. Both Sammy's drunkenness and his supposed nervous tendencies are implicated by police and health pro-fessionals in the novel, who seek to cast Sammy (not the police) as respon-sible for his condition. The doctor Sammy sees to verify his blindness refers to 'persons who entertain sightloss', a curious locution rendering a physical ailment into a social situation.[32] Like the efforts of the state officials to censor Sammy's speech, his 'sightloss' is a circumstance where he fails to measure up, yet another shortcoming in comparison to a normative, middle-class lifestyle – were he stronger mentally, he would not be blind, and by extension, were he of stronger character, he would not be poor and unemployed.

But Kelman shows Sammy's strength; he declines assistance, both from a 'rep' seeking to help him navigate state bureaucracy and from charities providing guide dogs, walking sticks, and so on. As Scott Hames has aptly noted, Sammy's refusal of compensation is in part a denial of a 'degraded, impersonal form of justice rooted in abstract equivalence'.[33] For our purposes here, what is important is the insight that seeking money as recompense for physical injury allows for monetary value, and therefore a limit, to be placed on a person's worth. Rejection of payment for damages equals rejection of a merit-based social system determined by class-based criteria. Moreover, the 'rep' Ally seeks to speak for Sammy, and is thereby 'Kelman's metaphor for a kind of naïve working-class novelist, one who aims to "represent" the lower classes to a middle-class audience and perhaps win redress for their sufferings'.[34] Like Patrick's brother Gavin in A *Disaffection*, Sammy does not require sympathy from those higher up the social hierarchy. Patrick recalls a table tennis match where 'he had been easing up and trying to let Gavin win and then suddenly he wasnt having any say on the matter, Gavin was fucking running him ragged'; throughout the novel we see Gavin squirming under the narrator's presumptions.[35] Gavin, and by extension Sammy and even the working class, do not need the patronising help of Patrick, Ally and prize judges. If in A *Disaffection* Kelman explores a sympathetic member of the culturally privileged class unable to resist its values, in *How late* he considers a character with no investment in that sphere.

Cairns Craig has advocated cultural activity 'which is about benefits neither tangible nor measurable', which resists the pressure to link use value and exchange value by declining to fulfil 'people's perceived requirements'.[36] From Patrick's feeling of 'life being exactly too much, that precise amount' to Sammy's escape from our view at novel's end, his existence 'in excess of what is narrated', Kelman upends notions of value.[37] By redefining which words contain value and who determines what is important, he offers a radical challenge to the literary canon and the economic structure it exists within. One can wonder why Kelman would be so willing, after his 1989 Booker no-show, to accept nominations and awards. Perhaps the radical redefinition of value he undertakes is to see the prize as Sammy would: 'The prize will be useful. I'm totally skint.'[38]

CHAPTER THREE

Kelman's Later Novels

Peter Boxall

This chapter will argue that James Kelman's novels of the twenty-first century – *Translated Accounts*, *You Have to be Careful in the Land of the Free*, and *Kieron Smith, boy* – collectively shape a new kind of political fiction. Their radicalism emerges from Kelman's earlier prose, and from the critical and literary traditions assimilated in previous writing, but the post-Booker novels none the less suggest a bold re-imagining of the role and scope of fiction in addressing contemporary political forms. If political fiction has tended to be understood, after the Frankfurt School, in terms of the distinction between autonomous and committed literary practice, then Kelman's recent work suggests ways of moving past this opposition, and towards a new form of political writing that blends a commitment to local political realities with a strikingly innovative narrative practice, and that refashions the relation between autonomy and commitment.

Both *Kieron Smith, boy* and *You Have to be Careful* extend the tradition of Glaswegian working-class fiction to which Kelman in part belongs, and partly as a result their political affiliations and operations feel at first sight more familiar.[1] Their political force stems both from their engagement with this tradition, and from their formally inventive testing of the limits of a certain kind of narrative perspective, the kind of interior monologue that was developed by the modernist avant-garde. When Jeremiah in *Careful* describes himself, repeatedly, as an 'unassimilatit' and 'nonintegratit' alien, he suggests a number of political positions at once. His refusal (or inability) to integrate in the 'land of the free' is part of the novel's broad satire on the capacity of the US to tolerate cultural difference in a period of xenophobic paranoia after 9/11; that he should express and experience his non-assimilation in a 'Skarrisch' dialect suggests that this critique of US hegemony is conducted from the perspective of a local culture and a local idiom that shapes and colours Jeremiah's thinking and his language. But the radical embeddedness of the narrative within Jeremiah's own head suggests that the alienation that he describes is a philosophical as well as a cultural one, that the narrative performs his incapacity to get outside the coils of his own exhausting interiority, as much as it does his failure to find himself at home in American freedom.

Both *Careful* and *Kieron* owe something to a tradition of realism which sets out to depict a cultural location of experience with great precision or authenticity. Both are also, however, indebted to an avant-garde tradition which traces a narrative interiority which breaks from 'empirical reality', in pursuit of what Theodor Adorno has called 'concrete historical reality' – the reality that Adorno finds in the collapsing inwards of Beckett's and Kafka's monologues. Their politics, then, arises both from a determination to maintain fidelity to local conditions and idioms – in an attempt to 'write back' to the centre that has some similarities to the postcolonial practices developed by writers such as Salman Rushdie – and from the inventiveness of their production of a narrative voice. *Translated Accounts*, however, seems to produce and require an entirely different kind of political rhetoric, and as a result might seem to develop a kind of praxis that is very different not only from Kelman's other novels of the decade, but of his œuvre more generally. This work does not locate itself in a recognisable social space at all, nor does it house itself within the secure confines of any particular narrative perspective. Rather, it moves across a range of protocols for the reporting or gathering of witness accounts, giving a picture of a violence and alienation that is utterly generalised and unlocated. The political task of this work is not to write back to a centre from a specific margin, or to find a language for a particular kind of social experience, but rather to suggest or articulate a collapse of the forms of sovereignty and subjecthood that have allowed for the very possibility of private experience and interior narration. These accounts resemble nothing so much as Beckett's *Fizzles*, translated to a world shaped by Hardt and Negri's empire rather than those of the European powers, in which the dissolution of Beckett's narrative practice into fizzles of prose velleity (entitled 'He is barehead', or 'I gave up before birth') is matched by the collapse of Kelman's located narratives into the computerised, translated languages of networked military administration (entitled 'if under false pretences', or 'who asks the question').

The different political categories and traditions to which these novels belong, then, are characterised by the way in which narrative agents are engaged with specific historical and cultural conditions, and by the possibilities for critique and transformation that arise from such engagement. Kieron and Jeremiah suggest a kind of cultural politics in that their idiom offers to reshape the language from within, to force written English to accommodate rhythms of speech and thought that have been excluded from the public sphere; the nameless narrators of *Translated Accounts* suggest the difficulty of any political action or identification under political conditions that are recognisable only in their anonymous generality. While Kieron and Jeremiah invent a singular language which arises from the movement of their thought, the nameless narrators of *Translated Accounts* remain buried somewhere beneath an unstyled prose, their words and thoughts translated and edited by an unrevealed bureaucracy. If there is a politics arising from *Translated Accounts*, then it might be suggested that it is a politics which presides over the end of politics, a kind of flat dystopian refusal of the political possibilities of fiction. But what is being argued here is that this separation, this kind of categorisation of political aesthetics, is precisely what these three novels taken together offer to rethink. The apparent sharpness of the distinction between them at the level of form belies a rich seam of shared concerns – with translation, with editing, with the temporality and spatiality of narration – that crosses the formal divide that separates them, and gestures towards a new category of political fiction.

Perhaps the most striking mark of this shared concern is the tendency for the formal distinctions themselves, between *Translated Accounts* on the one hand and *Kieron* and *Careful* on the other, to give way under pressure. Everything I have been saying about the novels so far assumes that narrative dispersal in *Translated Accounts* is set against an intense narrative focus or singularity in *Kieron* and *Careful*. One of the remarkable things about these novels, however, is that the very radicalism of their treatment of narrative perspective produces a kind of reversal, in which singularity becomes strangely bound up with multiplicity; the sealed narrating subject in *Kieron* and *Careful* betrays a peculiar continuity with the dispersed narrators of *Translated Accounts*. This reversal effect is at work throughout the three novels, but can be seen particularly sharply in the seventeenth passage in *Translated Accounts*, entitled 'split in my brain'. This 'account' gives witness to some kind of interrogation scene, in which the anonymous first-person narrator suffers a terrible but unspecified violence, as a result of which 'the back of the head was broken, my head', and 'a split had formed in my brain'.[2] This opening of a kind of cleaving in the mind suggests the splitting and fracturing of narrative perspective that is the most striking formal aspect of the novel. The compelling and disturbing thought that the 'back' of the narrator's head is 'broken', that the violence which saturates these texts has opened a rift in the sealed unit of the head itself, allows in a sense for the leakage of narrative identity and positioning, the loss of a stable subjecthood, to which the novel more generally attests. This kind of undoing or separating of the mind, indeed, strikes a perhaps surprising resonance with the poetry of Emily Dickinson, allowing a slant of nineteenth-century light into this scene of twenty-first century brutality and torture. The split that forms in the broken narrator's mind in *Translated Accounts* shares a seam with that cleft that opens in Dickinson's poetry in 1864:

I felt a Cleaving in my Mind –
As if my Brain had split –

I tried to match it – Seam by Seam –
But could not make them fit –

The thought behind, I strove to join
Unto the thought before –
But Sequence ravelled out of Sound –
Like Balls – upon a Floor – [3]

The extraordinary, almost unthinkable disorientation that Dickinson conjures here, in which the disjoining of thought from thought causes 'sequence'
to 'ravel out of sound', catches perfectly the unravelling of sequence and
sound in *Translated Accounts*. But what is striking about the experience of
cleaving, both in Kelman and in Dickinson, is that it bears out the uncanny
continuity between separation and fusion that is carried by the word itself.
The narrator in Kelman's novel experiences a distance and alienation from
his (her?) own thinking that feels like a consequence of the rift that has
opened at the back of the head. He thinks ungrammatically and nonsequen-
tially about the question of freedom – 'freedom not being a true freedom
which I knew even then. If based on a degree of exploitation.'[4] These
displaced thoughts, he admits, are 'self-evident things', but the intuition of
this evident contradiction between freedom and exploitation is a difficult
knowledge to own, he thinks, because it is a (translated) knowledge that
cannot quite fit in his broken mind, a 'knowledge that lay beyond the edge
of my brain'.[5] This strange unavailability of his own administered thought,
however, does not simply produce a distance from self, a leaking of thought
beyond the horizons of the cleft mind; rather it also produces and requires
a kind of falling inward, a fusing together of distance and proximity, a relo-
cation of the beyond to the within. The narrator says, either of himself or
of his interrogator, that 'His voice was at such a distance', but this sense of
remoteness leads him to move not only outwards, but also inwards towards
seclusion and interiority.[6] 'Soon', he says, 'I had entered into my own self.'
As he looks around him, he says that 'I stared way way beyond,' but the
cleaving in his mind configures the beyond as a within, allowing him to
conceive a 'method of inclosing myself in nothing but myself'.[7] 'I was staring
at the ceiling', he says, 'and it was as a mirror, I saw myself, staring out at
the mountains beyond.' 'The place itself', he says, 'was round me and inside
attempting to overthrow, take control.'[8]

The displaced, dispersed, broken narrators of *Translated Accounts*, then,
experience a peculiarly intense interiority as a function and a consequence of
their dispersal – the experience of translation, editing, and violent distance
from self is also an 'entering into my own self'. This cleaving at the boundary
in *Translated Accounts* – this sense that the thresholds of the novel are at once

open and closed – is what determines the singular kind of communication that occurs between Kelman's late novels, the continuity that crosses the sealed and porous horizons of all three works of the 2000s, and that opens on to a new fictional politics. The splitting that occurs, in fact, in 'split in my brain' finds a kind of echo in both *Kieron Smith, boy* and *You Have to be Careful*, as if the tension in *Translated Accounts* between singularity and multiplicity crosses the formal divide between the novels, playing itself out in an inverted reflection in the later two works. In both *Kieron* and *Careful*, the perhaps-dominant narrative effect conjures double-voicing from the insistence on an extreme monovocalism. Virtually every sentence in both novels exhibits this effect to some degree or other. Throughout *Kieron Smith, boy*, for example, the movement of Kieron's thought is followed with such suppleness, such intimacy, that the narrative finds itself paradoxically taken beyond itself, in the same way that the narrator in *Translated Accounts* encounters 'knowledge that lay beyond the edge of my brain'. Kieron's narration gives itself with an extraordinary seamlessness not only to other people – to his father, his brother, his granda – but also to animals, to boats, to things, as the apparent lack of any mediation of Kieron's thought leaves us unable to distinguish between his imagining or remembering of occurrences, and those occurrences themselves. Kieron describes a scene in which his mother and brother discover that their house has mice: 'My maw went potty and started greeting,' he says.

> Me and Mattie scattered them and chased them but we could not catch them and did not know what to do. My maw was shouting in a high voice. Ohh ohhh![9]

This peculiar giving over of the narrative voice to the cries of Kieron's mother suggests already the capacity of the narrative to transform an intimacy with Kieron's interiority into a kind of exteriority, as his voice becomes one with that of his mother. But as the narrative continues, these cries themselves become merged with or rhyme with others, suggesting a growing sense of narrative dispersal. A few pages later, Kieron tells a story about going to the river with his dad to see the boats. As he enters the scene in his imagination ('ye had to go round a corner and round a river-street and then back down and there was the river and the boat was there') he remembers the sound of the fog horns of the boats on the river, as he heard them from his bedroom.[10] 'Ye heard the horn sometimes', Kieron says

> and ye were in bed, it was creepy, ye were maybe asleep but ye still heard it, if it was coming out of nowhere, that was how it sounded, ooohhhhh ooohhhhh, ooohhhhh, ooohhhhh, oooooohhhhhhhhh, and a big low voice. Just creepy.[11]

This moment is a multiply occupied one, which pulls the narrative in a number of directions. The ooohhhhs of the boat, coming out of nowhere, catch at the ohhs of Kieron's mother remembered just previously, suggesting a kind of accent or idiom that the boat and the mother share, and this difficult, displacing rhyming adds to the other forms of dislocation that are at work here – the sense that the 'big low voice' of the boat has drowned out Kieron's own voice, the sense that the narrative lays the scene at the river over the scene in which Kieron lies in his bedroom, thinking of the river. And these delicately cloven, woven strands are given an extra twist when Kieron goes on to describe seeing a boat emerge from the fog, as he stands at the riverside with his dad:

> And the yellow was coming out, all bright through the fog, and it was all lights, ye could not even see the funnels or the top parts because with the fog all hiding it. But there it was it was the ship out from the fog, ooohhhhh ooohhhhh, it was the special one.[12]

As the boat slides into visibility, it gives rise to these cries, these 'ooohhhh's which are beautifully unreadable, at once the voice of the boat, the voice of the people at the quayside watching the boat, the cries of Kieron's mother as she flees from the mice, and the sound of Kieron himself, at the scene or looking back on the scene, marvelling at the specialness of a boat sliding yellowly out of the fog.

This kind of effect, this splicing of the single and the double, is at work in every sentence both of Kieron and of Careful, and in both novels this cleaving produces a remarkable fluidity, in which different geographies, and separate spatial and temporal narrative structures, enter into a new kind of proximity, a new kind of conjoint and disjunct configuration. In You Have to be Careful, as Jeremiah sits planted in a jazz bar on his last evening in 'Uhmerka', his mind wanders across times, places and accents, and as the narrative follows his thought it produces an extraordinary blending or melding of cultures and subject positions. Towards the end of the evening, Jeremiah finds himself in conversation with an American couple named Norman and Rita, and Jeremiah is 'blethering on', telling them stories about his job as a security guard. He remarks at one point that, as a 'wean', he had been told he should 'never comment to strangers except on particular issues', and remembers that

> My boss at the Security agency used to say something along the same lines [. . .] General conclusions are de rigueur in Security operations, that was what he telt me. Universal blethers lead to moral imperatives and naybody wants into that sort of stuff, especially in uniform. He said it with his ayn accent.[13]

This is a freighted moment in the novel, a moment at which Jeremiah recognises that his boss at the Security agency spoke with an accent, presumably 'Uhmerkan', that is at odds with Jeremiah's own rendering of the scene. Jeremiah's thinking his way into the language of his boss tends to remake it, to cast a 'Skarrischness' over it, just as the accounts in *Translated Accounts* are modelled and edited by invisible processes. The nature of the narrative structure in *Careful*, the absence of anything other than Jeremiah's perspective, means that this merging of Scottish and American, of boss and worker, produces a remarkably intimate kind of hybridity in which it becomes difficult or impossible to find the boundaries between places and between subject positions. A little while later in Jeremiah's conversation with Norman and Rita, Norman upbraids Jeremiah for his use of swear words. Jeremiah is telling them that gambling is a 'stupit stupit crazy mental fucking game', and Norman, we are told, sighs, and tells Jeremiah that his language is 'a little hard on the ears':

> I do apologize.
> You get excited, said Rita.
> Ye're right, I do.
> People use that language in Skallin? said Norman.[14]

Even though the narrative has taken the form of dialogue here, in which Jeremiah's memory or experience of the scene resembles omniscient narration, Norman's use of the word 'Skallin' reminds us that Jeremiah is translating here, that one must imagine another version of this conversation in which Norman speaks in his 'ayn accent' (whatever that is). As Jeremiah's own speech and thought is inflected by a range of Americanisms, so the America that he encounters is rephrased, insistently, as a kind of Scotland, as the 'land of the free' becomes strangely contiguous with the land of Jeremiah's birth, the land to which he is trying half-heartedly to return.

It is in *Kieron Smith, boy* that this kind of hybridity, this merging of different temporalities and geographies of narration, is at its most poetically and politically inventive. Here, as in *Translated Accounts* and *Careful*, the capacity to gather together disjoined spaces and subject positions produces at once a coming together and a kind of dispersal, a cleaving as destructive, in its way, as the split that opens in the narrator's head in *Translated Accounts*. This simultaneous gathering and dispersal expresses itself most delicately in the relation that is established between the narrator as narrator (Kieron addressing us as readers, from some unspecified time and place of narration) and the narrator as character (Kieron as a boy, climbing his rone-pipe, doing his round, or catching a fish). The classic form that this relation takes is perhaps most clearly and influentially modelled in Charles Dickens's novel

Great Expectations, in which Pip as character, lost in the uncertainties and the naïveties of youth, slowly grows towards the maturity and wisdom of Pip as narrator, whose ethical clarity can be felt as a counterweight to his character's confusion throughout the narrative. The model, of course, is adapted time and time again, and in the service of various aesthetic regimes – by Proust in *À la recherche*, by Beckett in his middle trilogy, by Don DeLillo in his great wheeling novel *Underworld*. But, in *Kieron Smith, boy*, Kelman takes this model to the limits of its possibility, forging in the process a new kind of narrative practice. The immediacy of the narrative, its total immersion in the moving thought of the narrator, leads one to imagine, for large parts of the novel, that there is no distinction here between the place of narration and the narrated place. There is no narrative frame that establishes such a distinction, and no temporal plot that takes us from character towards narrator. Rather, for the most part, narrator and character occupy almost the same thought, as if they are woven into each other's minds. Take for example the wonderful, harrowing scene in which Kieron borrows his brother's bicycle and has it stolen by a 'man':

> But it was just a man done it. A man done it and was a complete thief. I would never do nothing ever ever again, just never ever, never never ever. If something ever happened to me and was ever ever good. Nothing ever could be ever again. If God would save me. It was not my fault. I would make a promise.[15]

Here, the narrative mood, the telling of the story of the stolen bicycle, folds into a continuous present, in which the prose is caught completely in the spirals of Kieron's panic and despair. It is not simply that the narrative reproduces with great immediacy Kieron's overwhelming misery – caught with wonderful precision in the repeated 'never never ever'. What is striking here is that the future from which this scene might conceivably be narrated is banished with astonishing vehemence, leaving us in a narrated present which divorces itself from the flow of time, a present in which 'nothing ever could be ever again'. But despite this tendency for the narrative to become immersed in the scenes it narrates, the figure of the narrator, of some older Kieron who no longer inhabits the language or the body or the mind of Kieron as character, insistently and repeatedly asserts itself, producing an odd sense of evacuation from the scenes that are evoked with such a vivid presence. Even the first sentence of the novel suggests such an evacuation. The novel opens with the assertion that 'In the old place the river was not far from our street,' declaring from the outset that the scenes in the Glasgow tenement that make up the first sections of the novel belong to an older time, that for all their presence they are in the past, remembered from a vantage point in which Kieron has already left the city, is already marooned in the schemes.[16] As the narrative continues, this switching between a continuous present and a narrated past becomes ever more fluid, a kind of dance in which narrator and narrated join and separate in the moving breath of the sentence. Take the opening scene in which Kieron catches a fish:

> If a fish came by ye saw it and just waited till it came in close. If it just stayed there over yer hands, that was how ye were waiting. It was just looking about. What was it going to do? Oh be careful if ye do it too fast, if yer fingers just move and even it is just the totiest wee bit. Its tail whished and it was away or else it did not and stayed there, so if ye grabbed it and ye got it and it did not get away. So that was you, ye caught one.[17]

Here, the narrative enters and slips clear of the scene it narrates with a beautiful sinuousness, opening and closing the distance between narrator and narrated in obedience to a snaky, slippery rhythm. The narrative mood is set with Kieron's description or remembrance of a time when he would catch fish in the 'old place' ('the park had a great pond in it', he says, 'with paddleboats and people sailed model yachts. Ye caught fish in it too').[18] The opening of the above quotation – 'If a fish came by' – suggests that the fishing we are imagining here is not a specific scene, but the kind of fishing that Kieron used generally to do. But as the scene moves on, the fish shifts from the general to the specific, no longer the kind of fish that Kieron used to try to catch, but an actual fish, sliding into Kieron's grasp, just as his remembered boat slides into visibility out of the fog. 'What was it going to do?' and 'Oh be careful' plunge us back into the scene of the catching itself, in which the fish is not yet caught, in which the delicate, subtle action of trapping this moving creature requires of the narrator a stealth and speed of movement rather than an accurate recall, a kind of movement that is registered in the syntax itself, which seeks to catch at its own fugitive prey. And this takes us to the sentence in which experience and reportage, the remembered past and the continuous present, are brought side by side, into a kind of resonance which seems to require a new tense, to place before and after, here and there, into a new kind of relation to each other: 'Its tail whished and it was away or else it did not and it stayed there, so if ye grabbed it and ye got it and it did not get away.' Here 'its tail whished' produces the sudden accelerating movement of the fish in two time frames at once, both in the present and in the past. It can be paraphrased both as something like 'sometimes the fish would swish its tail and get away and sometimes it would not,' and as 'be careful, because the fish might swish its tail, and then it will get away' – and the narrative does not allow us to prioritise the one over the other, creating a strange, stretched merging of past, present and future. The last sentence, 'so that was you, ye caught one', has a certain bathos to it, as the narrator resumes his distance from the scene, denying the lived excitement of 'it did not get away', but it does nothing to protect the narrator from this singular involvement with the scene he narrates. The narrator's retrospective distance from his narrative has already, on this first page, been annihilated, and the rest of the novel takes place in that strange, untensed continuity that is summoned here in the catching of a fish.

It is this continuity that is shared by all three of Kelman's post-2000 novels, and which summons a new kind of thinking about the writing of commitment. This continuity does not suggest a community to which Kelman's writing strives to give a voice. Indeed the forms of collectivity that are imagined in these works are closely, intimately entwined with a sundering, a cloven alienation between narrator and narrated, between here and there, between Scotland and America. These novels are built around the seam that Dickinson discovers, in 1864, between broken sequence and fractured identities. In *Kieron Smith, boy*, as in Dickinson's poem, the failure to find a join between 'the thought behind' and 'the thought before' produces a 'cleaving in the mind', a collapse of the machine that produces sequential meaning. The difference that opens and closes between narrator and narrated in *Kieron Smith, boy* produces a split between self and self that breaks the novel, leaving it open, as in *Translated Accounts*, somewhere at the back. Looking at a photograph of himself, or thinking of the seductive possibility that, secretly, he might be a 'pape' (a Roman Catholic), Kieron comes back time and again to his inability to match himself to himself, 'Seam by Seam'. Looking at his face, or thinking of his face, he wonders 'if it was me'. 'I could not see if it was me', he thinks. 'Ye thought ye knew your face', he says, speaking to us, speaking to himself, 'but when ye tried to see it in yer head ye could not.'[19] The breath of difference from self that the narrative finds in the most intimate expression of self means that one can never inhabit one's face completely – never, never, ever – that one always feels that awful opening at the back made by state violence in *Translated Accounts*, the opening that means one is always perhaps another. 'Maybe', Kieron thinks as he listens to his mother saying his name – as he hears and remembers his mother say 'Oh Kieron' – 'Maybe I was another boy.'[20]

This production, in Kelman's recent writing, of a difference from self in the most intimate heartland of the self, destabilises any simple sense that he is giving here an authentic account of a specific subject position, or that he is seeking to give a voice to a previously marginalised community or historical experience. He is not writing back from margin to centre here, not least because his writing produces a wonderfully eloquent testimony to the stubborn refusal of thinking and writing, remembering and imagining, to stay confined within the boundaries of any subject position, or of any historical or geographical field, either on the margins or at the centre. But this poetic exploration of the difficulty of finding a position from which to speak, or a face which one might inhabit, never amounts to an abandonment of political commitment. *Kieron Smith, boy, You Have to be Careful* and *Translated Accounts* all engage with forms of political and sociohistorical reality, and all explore the means by which such forms are experienced, remembered and recorded. What results is a forensic examination of the forces and pressures that are exerted on the contemporary imagination as it strives to conjure a sense of personhood from the conflicting violences – national, postnational, economic – that dismember us. These novels produce some of the sharpest analyses we have of the ways that such forces position us at the dawn of the twenty-first century; but they also offer one of the most delicate poetic responses to such forces, as the possibility of a kind of becoming emerges, untensed and almost unworded, from the very violence that has cloven the subject apart. It is with the broken mind of *Translated Accounts* that these novels think their way towards that 'knowledge' that 'lay beyond the edge of my brain'.[21]

CHAPTER FOUR

Kelman and the Short Story

Adrian Hunter

In 1906, G. K. Chesterton published a biography of Charles Dickens. It was a pessimistic book in which the author compared the state of British fiction in his own day to that of Dickens's generation and found it wanting. Of particular concern to Chesterton was the vogue among his contemporaries for the short story, then enjoying a remarkable elevation in status and popularity, largely as a result of the boom in the late-Victorian magazine trade. The rise of the short story, he contended, was nothing less than the symptom of a culture in crisis: 'Our modern attraction to short stories is not an accident of form; it is the sign of a real sense of fleetingness and fragility; it means that existence is only an impression, and, perhaps, only an illusion.'[1] Taking a swipe at the whole field, from the urban realism of Arthur Morrison to the imperial fantasies of Rudyard Kipling, Chesterton condemned the turn to the short story as a retreat into smallness, a betrayal of the reading public, and an unconscionable abandonment on the part of writers of those 'ultimate and enduring' values that had made possible the Victorian novelist's art.[2]

It is difficult now to see what Chesterton was worried about, so emphatically has the novel reinstalled itself at the centre of our literary culture. But while his comments may sound feverish to modern ears, they do assert something highly relevant to the study of James Kelman, namely that form is more than just the vessel in which content arrives, and can itself be an expression (an embodiment, one might say) of cultural and political value. Ever since Cairns Craig's celebrated 1993 article 'Resisting Arrest',[3] Kelman criticism has focused on the question of the relationship of content to form; but oddly, it has failed to address the most obvious formal gesture Kelman makes in his fiction, the choice between novel and short story – surely as significant an expression of artistic preference as any he has shown around narrative language (the main concern of Craig's essay).[4] In common with the modernist writers he is fond of citing, Kelman approaches the short story not as a condensed, attenuated or unelaborated novel, but as a form otherwise resourced and otherwise expressive; in the words of the Irish writer Elizabeth Bowen, he regards its 'shortness' as a 'positive' quality rather than a matter merely of 'non-extension'.[5] For Kelman, the short story is a genre in its own right, a separate event from the novel, governed by distinct aesthetic principles and capable of performing its own cultural work.

I mentioned a moment ago Kelman's affinity with the modernists, and this I would suggest is where we need to begin our encounter with his short stories. In a number of interviews and essays, Kelman has spoken of the significance for the development of his own fictional practice of American modernists such as Ernest Hemingway, Sherwood Anderson, Gertrude Stein and Katherine Anne Porter – all of them writers drawn to experiment in various ways with the short form (indeed, Hemingway's inclusion in the modernist canon at all is largely as a result of the stories he produced early in his career).[6] What characterises all these writers' work is a radical de-emphasis of plot, action and dramatic incident in favour of a focus on the subjective, experiential moment. Markedly inconclusive, more concerned to render the passing impression than to shape eventful sequences of action towards determinate ends, modernist stories favour ellipsis and structural aperture, open endings and interrogative impasses. As Katherine Mansfield, another writer who dedicated her career to short stories, described: 'What the writer does is not so much to *solve* the question but to *put* the question [. . .] There must be the question put. That seems to me a very nice dividing line between the true and the false writer.'[7] By rejecting the artifice of plot, the modernists hoped to render more faithfully the quality of human experience and the motility of the perceiving mind. For the same reasons, modernist stories tend to eschew any trace of omniscient narration, preferring instead to confine narrative point-of-view within character consciousness, either through first-person narration or the deployment of free indirect style.

Kelman's responsiveness to the poetics of the modernist text is key to his achievement as a writer. Reading through his criticism and self-commentary one finds repeated references to his absorption of modernist thinking and his attempts to adapt it to his own fictional practice. In a 1985 interview with Duncan McLean, for example, he gives the following account of the significance of the concrete 'fact' in his work:

> In setting out the fact, you have set out the danger, because the danger is inherent within the fact, you know. I mean the fact really itself is hair-raising; if you can put forward that fact, then you can put forward the hair-raising-ness of the experience, you know, which is why I go after all those wee effects, such as no abstractions – everything's concrete. It's only through the concrete that you actually get the terror, you know. [William] Carlos Williams again. Just state the thing, don't think in terms of ideas; if you get the thing properly, then you've got it. If you state those terrible things that go on in a factory, if you just put them down, then you'll get the horror of it, you don't have to say 'This is horrible.' Just state it properly, and it's there.[8]

Such remarks clearly situate Kelman's fictional aesthetic within the modernist imaginary. His terms of reference here draw on the manifesto of the Imagist movement (with which William Carlos Williams was associated), which prescribed that poetry should avoid abstraction and deal instead in concrete images. As F. S. Flint put it in his 1913 'Three Rules', the priority was a 'direct treatment of the "Thing" whether subjective or objective', a doctrine elaborated by Ezra Pound in terms very similar to Kelman's own:[9]

> An 'Image' is that which presents an intellectual and emotional complex in an instant of time [. . .]
> It is the presentation of such a 'complex' instantaneously which gives that sense of sudden liberation; that sense of freedom from time limits and space limits; that sense of sudden growth, which we experience in the presence of the greatest works of art.
> [. . .]
> Use no superfluous word, no adjective which does not reveal something.
> Don't use such an expression as 'dim lands of *peace.*' It dulls the image. It mixes an abstraction with the concrete. It comes from the writer's not realizing that the natural object is always the *adequate* symbol.
> Go in fear of abstractions.[10]

A number of aesthetic principles join together in this list: not just the treatment of the image and the concrete term, but an aversion to the abstract, which is really a failure to recognise the extent to which the object itself 'is always the *adequate* symbol'. This is doctrine both for Pound and for Kelman. Abstraction equates to a superintendent discursive authority in the text; it represents an attempt by the writer to direct the reader, to infiltrate an explanatory, even coercive voice into the text, and a failure thereby to present the object on its own terms, to let it speak for itself.

Characteristic of Kelman's stories is their 'straight concreteness' in which, as the author himself puts it, 'there's only facts being stated, there's no [. . .] value judgement.'[11] In common with his modernist forebears, particularly Hemingway and Stein, Kelman organises his conspicuously 'plotless' stories around quotidian incidents that are not elaborated to any conclusion or embedded within larger sense-making narrative structures; events unfold sequentially, in the manner one would expect of realist fiction, but the sense of meaningful *consequence* arising from them is scrupulously suppressed. This tendency is particularly marked in the one-page stories that compose the early collection *Short Tales from the Night Shift* (1978). 'Learning the Story', for example, captures a brief encounter between an unnamed narrator and an old woman sitting beneath a bridge over the River Kelvin in Glasgow. The woman sings and plays the mouthorgan and smokes Capstan full-strength cigarettes. The narrator tries to engage her in conversation:

I always liked that tune, I told her. She struck a match and lighted a cigarette. She flicked the match a distance and it landed with smoke still rising from it. Drawing the shopping bag in between her raised knees she inhaled deeply, exhaled staring at her boots. Cheerio then, I said. I paced on beneath the bridge aware of my footsteps echoing. The lady wore specs and had a scarf wrapped round her neck. Her nose was bony. Her skirt may have showed under the hem of her coat. When she was playing the mouthorgan she had moved slightly from foot to foot. Her coat was furry.[12]

Reminiscent of the brief 'intertexts' in Hemingway's In Our Time, this passage (which concludes the 'tale') shows Kelman experimenting with effects of compression and ellipsis in much the way that the modernists did. It is a minor piece, no question, but it does reveal the origins of techniques that characterise his mature style: the suppression not just of an evaluative register to mediate the details of what is being described, but of the grammatical connective tissue we normally look for in continuous prose to orientate one sentence or clause in relation to the next. The unevaluated facticity in which this passage dissipates, and the way it eschews any trace of authoritative discursive imposition, are early instances of what will become a fully developed theory of narrative for Kelman.

What Kelman unquestionably learned from modernist story writers was the power of restricted articulation and elliptical narrative structures in the short story – that less can be more, that meaning can be liberated rather than curtailed by discursive reticence and abbreviation. However, his determined refusal, evident throughout his essays and interviews, to divorce form from content (or in terms he might prefer, art from politics) forces us to consider the wider implications of his engagement with the modernist aesthetic. For as a committed realist, Kelman's priority has been the development of a fictional practice that faithfully represents working-class reality, rather than evading it under the guise of 'literature'. His stories may narrate the surface of things, and there may be a lack of discernible significance in the events they retail, but that is Kelman's way of remaining within the world he creates, rather than assuming a superior viewing position outside it. His attraction to the short story is to a form that strips away the generic falsifications of plot, narrative determinacy and structural coherence, a form that in its very brevity tends towards the fragmentary, inconclusive and atomistic – a desaturated and ambiguous textual event perfectly calibrated to the portrayal of a working class that has, in Cairns Craig's words, itself 'become atomized, fragmented [. . .] isolated'.[13] Far from being the handmaiden to his novels, the short story is the form that best accommodates Kelman's artistic and political vision.

In Not not while the giro (1983), the first major collection of his stories to be published in Britain, Kelman manages to harness the techniques of modernist

narrative to a wider political purpose and commitment to realism. Reading
through the stories, one is struck, yes, by their indebtedness to an earlier
generation of writers, but also, and more significantly, by the ways in which
Kelman is able to utilise interrogative, open-ended story forms to capture
the experiential reality of working-class life. The stories are at once formally
beguiling, socially authentic and ideologically challenging. As an example,
consider 'Acid', a short narrative of the sort Kelman likes to intersperse
between longer stories in all his collections. Here it is entire:

> In this factory in the north of England acid was essential. It was contained in
> large vats. Gangways were laid above them. Before these gangways were made
> completely safe a young man fell into a vat feet first. His screams of agony were
> heard all over the department. Except for one old fellow the large body of men
> was so horrified that for a time not one of them could move. In an instant this
> old fellow who was also the young man's father had clambered up and along the
> gangway carrying a big pole. Sorry Hughie, he said. And then ducked the young
> man below the surface. Obviously the old fellow had had to do this because only
> the head and shoulders – in fact, that which had been seen above the acid was
> all that remained of the young man.[14]

It is a beguiling text, much of its power deriving from the detachment and
lack of an evaluative register in the narrative voice, given what it purports
to depict. However, Kelman is not playing epistemological games with us
here; rather he is attempting to convey by that very sense of detachment the
alienation integral to a particular kind of working-class experience. The key
here is the word 'obviously' with which the final sentence begins, because
that adverb breaks down the illusion of consensus between the reader and the
impersonal narrator. We are bound to ask in what sense it is 'obvious' that the
father should act in the way he does. Once we ask that question, we find ourselves drawn towards a much larger story to do with work, or more precisely
with the sort of industrial labour to which particularly men, working-class
men, find themselves committed. It is the presence of this extrinsic narrative,
whose trace is everywhere in the details of the story, that prevents us from
regarding the image of the bobbing head and shoulders, or the father's emotionless reaction to the death of his son, as so much unreality, or even surreal-
ity, embedded as these details are within a specific socio-cultural actuality: a
factory in the north of England in which working-class men perform dangerous unregulated labour in the service of capital. Like Bertolt Brecht, Kelman
makes us conscious of the superstructural economic forces at play behind this
passing human drama, so that we are forced, for example, to consider the
curious indifference and sense of resignation in the father, not as the reaction
of an individual as such, but as the emanation of a class condition, of the lot
of those trapped on the wrong side of the labour-capital equation.

Throughout *Not not while the giro* we encounter stories that live this sort of double life: oblique, elliptical realist narratives that function as vectors of a greater social condition. Kelman's technique is to infiltrate that larger story into the narrative by disturbances in the language or in details in the surface events of the drama. 'He knew him well', 'The bevel' and 'The chief thing about this game', to take just three examples from the book, work in a similar way to 'Acid' by gesturing towards socio-cultural or political contexts of which the surface stories remain scrupulously inexpressive and imperceptive. 'He knew him well' takes the form of a conversation between the narrator and an old man in a pub. Their topic is a mutual acquaintance, old Dennis, who has committed suicide by cutting his wrist. This revelation is shocking when it comes, but straight away Kelman complicates the dramatic 'twist' by shifting our focus outward and away from Dennis's fate and on to something else. Here is how the story ends:

> 'Yeh . . .' The old guy nodded after a moment, then added, 'And the eating, it said in the paper . . .'
> 'That's right. The doctor, he said old Dennis couldn't have been eating for nearly a week beforehand.'
> 'Bloody fool,' he sighed. 'He should've ate. That's one thing you should do is eat. I take something every day, yeh, make sure of that. You got to. A drop of soup's good you know.'
> I ordered two more drinks just on the first bell, we stayed silent, smoking then drinking, until I finished and rose and said, 'Well, I'm off. See you again.'
> 'Yeh,' he muttered, staring into his glass. He shook his head, 'Old Dennis should've ate eh!'[15]

Up until this point the conversation has been about Dennis's past life as the speaker and the old man speculate on what may have led to his suicide. But with the revelation that he had starved the distance between the old man and the narrator on the one hand, and Dennis on the other, is suddenly reduced and the story dramatically reframed. The difference between the old man and Dennis is no longer that of survivor and victim; they are both victims of the same structural impoverishment. The opening of this portal in the story forces us to question just what did kill old Dennis. The old man's final remark, that Dennis should have eaten, is the self-protective, self-validating sentiment of the survivor, but it is inadequate as an explanation; nor does it amount to a remedy for what ails their like. In this sense the story resists the old man's closing statement; as with 'Acid' we are drawn away from the simple attribution of individual suffering to individual failing by the adumbration of social and economic forces bearing down upon the lives of working-class people.

'He knew him well' is an excellent example of Kelman's painstaking portrayal of the complex discursive and behavioural protocols that dominate working-class culture. For many readers, of course, this is what gives his stories such a compelling sense of authenticity. However, Kelman is also concerned with the ways in which these protocols function to obscure from the working class the truth of the conditions under which they live and labour; and it is in this respect that the old man's closing remark in 'He knew him well' is a mistake, a misrecognition of what really killed Dennis. We see this kind of elaborate misrecognition throughout *Not not while the giro*, particularly in the stories that take place in industrial work settings. In both 'The bevel' and 'The chief thing about this game', for example, the male characters observe highly developed behavioural and communicative protocols in respect of one another and the hierarchy of capital and labour as it exists in the workplace; but these protocols, whether connected with the work itself or with the diversionary activities of drinking, smoking and betting, also serve to immobilise the characters, to the extent that they remain incapable of resisting, challenging or concerting themselves to alter the conditions that oppress them.

As these readings suggest, Kelman's stories present a working class that is powerless, sundered, and eventually incapable of effecting change or any sort of social renewal. His subject is not the traditional (often romanticised) consolidated industrial working class of the mid-twentieth century, but 'the workless and the homeless, the casually and menially employed, the cadgers and the dodgers, in short the powerless marginalized section of the working class.'[16] It is a recurrent feature of his stories that characters remain unconscious of the wider perspective upon their condition that is made available to the reader through the text's ambiguities and ruptures. In part this is a reflection of Kelman's fidelity to realism – his wish to represent a class fraction as it really exists, 'atomized and dispossessed [. . .] desperate and [. . .] displaced';[17] it is also arguably a product of his encounter with the anglophone modernists and with Kafka, whose 'avoidance of relativistic, value-laden language' allowed for a representation of reality that was functionally free of bias.[18] Yet it is easy to see how one might criticise Kelman's work on these very same grounds. For by estranging his characters from any sense of community, presenting them as monads, solitary entities incapable of meaningful connection with those around them, Kelman perversely indulges in what Willy Maley terms an 'artistic individualism' which is at odds with the values he otherwise espouses: 'As a writer,' Maley argues, 'Kelman wants to maintain close links with his roots, his origins, his culture, his working-class background, yet the characters he creates find themselves out on a limb, isolated from the communities from which they arise.'[19]

It is a criticism that carries particular resonance in respect of the short story which, I have been suggesting, attracts Kelman precisely because of its atomistic, discontinuous quality. The Marxist critic Georg Lukács's critique of modernism can help clarify the issue here. For Lukács, the modernist text's tendency to present a 'superficial [. . .] fortuitous sequence of isolated static pictures' rather than explore the inner 'vital relations' and 'transformational possibilities' of social life, is the mark of its retreat from the moral challenges that advanced capitalist culture posed.[20] By offering merely a spectacle, a 'static apprehension of reality', modernism, Lukács argues, effectively transformed social ills of alienation and fragmentation into aesthetic virtues.[21] Something similar could be argued about Kelman's stories, namely that in their very abbreviation and lack of expressive fulfilment they mark a formal surrender to the oppressive logic of the capitalist metanarrative, forsaking any attempt to provide a coherent alternative to it.

This argument makes sense when one considers the extent to which Kelman's short stories seem to be preoccupied with stasis, paralysis and inconsequence. Many of the stories in *Greyhound for Breakfast* (1987) and *The Burn* (1991) depict working-class characters, mostly men, trapped in scenarios of perpetual deferral, unable to effect change or, even, to act. The prevailing temperament of Kelman's stories in both these collections is subjunctive; they are studies in suspended agency that by their brevity and lack of narrative fulfilment seem to embody the very sense of isolation and defeat they depict. '[T]here are things needing doing,' says the narrator of 'of the spirit':

> there are things needing doing I know I know I know it well but cant just bring myself to do them it isnt even as though there is that something that I can bring myself to do for if that was true it would be there I would be there and not having to worry about it [. . .][22]

More than a failure to act the narrator suffers from a failure to *know* how to act; and it is this sort of compound disability – cognitive, perceptual, physical, sexual, material – that characterises the majority of Kelman's protagonists. The internal language of these characters is stricken with a chronic provisionality; any statement they make which approaches the status of assertion is quickly hedged around with modal qualifiers or dispersed in self-doubt and circularity. 'That would be fine if he could just do that,' thinks the title character of 'Old Francis', 'But he couldnt, he couldnt do it'[23] – a sentiment that epitomises the Kelmanesque suffering male, from the demotic street mugger of 'The one with the dog' ('I'd just tell them to fuck off; away and fuck I'd tell them, that's what I'd say if it was me')[24] to the sex abuse victim of 'Pictures', suspended in an 'eternity of decision-making'[25] while those around him, from the Hollywood director of the 'picture' he is watching, to the murderer on the screen, to the man who abused him as a boy, inflict upon him assaultive narratives of sex, violence and domination, his internalisation of which renders him powerless either to resist or to escape.

Despite the fact that the majority of the twenty-one first-person narrators of *The Good Times* (1998) are materially better placed than those of the
earlier stories (in so far as they are in work, members of families, and partici-
pating, however problematically, in mainstream consumer society), Kelman
continues to dramatise scenarios of estrangement, disconnection, and political and emotional disaffection. The book is replete with narrators in motion
through populated social, familial and urban spaces, yet isolated within their
own subjective predicaments. They may register otherness and the need for
human exchange, but for the most part they remain islanded; as the narrator
of 'Oh my darling' puts it, with a nod to Samuel Beckett, 'whatever there is
left, it mostly takes place inside my skull.'[26] In 'Some thoughts that morning',
the narrator is a commuter travelling to work on a crowded Glasgow subway
train, but despite the proximity of many other people, whose socio-economic
or class status is not dissimilar to his own, he nevertheless feels himself
'not really involved in "the world" except perhaps by association, indirect
association'.[27] 'Some thoughts that morning' is Kelman's take on what was,
in the nineteenth century, a popular sub-genre of the short story: the tale
of the travelling coincidence, where strangers brought together in the car-
riage of a train become involved, briefly and tantalisingly, in one another's
lives. In Kelman's version, the motion of the train that creates inadvertent
physical contact between the passengers (a fixture of the Victorian genre
and the starting point for intrigue and interaction) is feared because 'the
outcome would prove awkward',[28] while the gaze of another person has the
power 'to force others into psychic turmoil'.[29] The narrator's response, his
only act of volition, is to submit to these conditions and turn his gaze to the
ground: 'I had done it before and would do it again, I could always do it again.
There are these amazing escapes and we give them to each other, despite
everything.'[30]

Arguably the most striking embodiment of urban male disaffection and
dispossession in all of Kelman's work is to be found in the narrator of 'Not
not while the giro', an unemployed man in more senses than one, whose
convoluted internal register cancels all possibility of action. 'Something must
be done,'[31] he avers, yet what ensues is *undoing* – or at least it would, were he
only able to undo:

> Suicide can be contemplated. Alright. I might have contemplated it. Or maybe
> I only imagined it, I mean seriously considered it. Or even simply and without
> the seriously. In other words I didnt contemplate suicide at all. I probably
> regarded the circumstances as being ideal. Yet in my opinion[32]

There is a simulacrum of analytic process here, an attempt to chase down
the fact of the matter. Yet this is thinking that issues in the cancellation of

what is thought. In a pattern characteristic of Kelman's monologists, the narrator begins with a proposition only to saw off the branch on which it sits, so that by the time we reach the final, abortive sentence it is unclear what assertion the adversative 'Yet in my opinion' seeks to rebut. Meanwhile the inconsequential quality of the narrator's thought is reflected in a fragmented, non-sequential narrative structure that disperses any impression of unity or coherence.

Read this way, 'Not not while the giro' would seem to exemplify Willy Maley's charge that Kelman is preoccupied with dramatising a monadic 'individualism' that re-inscribes, rather than counteracts, the very ideology that produces social atomism and isolation in the first place. However, Kelman's story is highly interrogative and one could equally well argue that it offers a critique rather than a reinforcement of the values Maley identifies. Consider this passage, for example:

> Taking everything into consideration the time may be approaching when I shall begin regularly paid, full-time employment. My lot is severely trying. For an approximate age I have been receiving money from the state. I am obliged to cease this malingering and earn an honest penny. Having lived in this fashion for so long I am well nigh unemployable and if I were an Industrial Magnate or Captain of Industry I would certainly entertain doubts as to my capacity for toil. I am an idle goodfornothing. A neerdowell. The workhouse is too good for the likes of me. I own up. I am incompatible with this Great British Society. My production rate is less than atrocious. An honest labouring job is outwith my grasp.[33]

In what sense is the narrator 'incompatible' with British society? In the economic sense: he is not a producer, a labourer, or an earner – not a viable economic unit, in other words. The challenge of the story is to see beyond whatever repulsion, pity or amusement the narrator's admissions may provoke in us to the structure of values that creates that repulsion, pity or amusement at a man who fails to work. The challenge here is comparable to that in Herman Melville's great tale of work and money, 'Bartleby, the Scrivener', where the title character's modest refusal to participate in the normative practices of capitalist society leads to his estrangement, incarceration and death. Like Kelman's narrator, Bartleby is designed to frustrate and infuriate. But the wider intention of Melville's text was that readers should reflect on the reasons for that frustration, and by that come to recognise the extent to which they had, in place of their common humanity, internalised the value system of capitalism – to the extent even that they struggled to accommodate a character unable or unwilling to function economically.

Something comparable is argued by Douglas Gifford, who regards the very uneventfulness of Kelman's stories as a challenge to the 'assumption[s] of a

privileged "Eng Lit"', and by extension to 'the middle-class reader' to 'empa-
thise sufficiently to flesh out the possibilities' of the narrative.[34] It is an idea
which returns us to the modernists and the power of elliptical indirection in
making the reader feel something more than they understand. Except that
Kelman's engagement with modernist aesthetics is, if one follows Gifford's
trail, in service of something more tangible and politically responsive than
'feeling'; it is, as Gifford suggests, a means of circumventing a dominant
value system. The attraction of this argument is that it provides another
articulation of the relationship between form and ideological function. That
is to say, the formal characteristics of Kelman's interrogative stories – their
'plotlessness', narrative deficits and expressive curtailments – come to be read
not as privations but as gestures of resistance to the ideological entailments of
power, authority and law. 'Shortness', to return to Elizabeth Bowen, becomes
a 'positive' quality.

Such a reading helps us to make sense of texts like 'Sunday papers' or
'The wean and that': narratives in which Kelman almost entirely suppresses
dramatic incident or any sense of structural resolution or closure. Just as 'Not
not while the giro' exposes our susceptibility to the subliminal structures of
capitalist ideology, so these texts challenge the expectations and assumptions we harbour concerning 'story' and narrative. In their very refusal to
manufacture any illusion of unity or dramatic purpose from the events they
retail, these stories force us, if we are to take anything from them at all, to find
other reasons for reading. They are 'anti-stories' of the sort Kelman finds in
Kafka: texts that '[create] the conditions for a "story"', but then exercise the
'ultimate possibility' and 'negate it'.[35] And as ever for Kelman, such negation
carries political, not just aesthetic weight. As he put it in a 1989 interview:
'The whole idea of the big dramatic event, of what constitutes "plot", only
assumes that economic security exists.'[36] In both content and form, the
stories seek to transcend the structures – ideological as well as narrative – that
capitalism would impose upon us.

Whether one concludes that Kelman's treatment of the short story marks
a capitulation or a creative resistance to the economic, social and cultural
conditions of the age – and Kelman himself might argue it either way – the
important thing is to recognise the role that the short form has played in the
production of his literary *and* political identities.

CHAPTER FIVE

Kelman's Critical and Polemical Writing

Mia Carter

What I try to do, he said, in the classroom I mean, is just make the weans angry. And other folk as well; I try to make them angry. That includes relations! [. . .] Because making them angry's a start. That's something. Even just making them angry.

A Disaffection[1]

war . . . war . . .
mi seh lissen
oppressin man
hear what I say if yu can
wi have
a grevious blow fi blow
[. . .]
wi hav a plan
soh lissen man
get ready fi tek some blows

Linton Kwesi Johnson, 'All Wi Doin Is Defendin'[2]

In his acceptance speech for the 1994 Booker Prize, James Kelman situated his work within a specific context linking art, politics and community:

There is a literary tradition to which I hope my work belongs. I see it as part of a much wider process, or movement towards decolonisation and self-determination: it is a tradition that assumes two things, 1) the validity of indigenous culture, and 2) the right to defend it in the face of attack. It is a tradition premised on a rejection of the cultural values of imperial or colonial authority, offering a defence against cultural assimilation [. . .] my culture and my language have the right to exist, and no one has the authority to dismiss that right.[3]

This 'defence' of Kelman's art and worldview was interpreted as a provocative attack. Kelman recalls the immediate reaction from the ceremony audience:

> They hated what I was saying and most of them were out for my blood when the press conference began. The first question that was asked was 'Why do you hate the English?' The journalist who asked could hardly conceal his anger, he was trembling.[4]

The speech was not televised, but was published in several newspapers the following week.[5] The *Sunday Times* headline typifies Kelman's frequent portrayal as a wild renegade or literary street-fighter: 'Kelman lines up his next shot.'[6]

If Kelman has occasionally lived up to this billing (typically when being interviewed), he has also found humour in his bellicose media image. On being asked if he had ever felt tempted to show up on hostile critics' doorsteps (as the English novelist Jeanette Winterson once famously did), Kelman remarked that he 'would have needed a machine gun!' in order to counter-attack the legions of critics who railed against *How late it was, how late* (see Chapter 2).[7] This chapter aims to examine both the anger and the warmth of Kelman's polemical writing, its complexity as well as its crudeness. Media stereotypes aside, Kelman's unswerving anger is real, and deserves attention as an important factor in his writing. As we shall see, his entrenched oppositional stance is serious, strategic, and rooted in the Marxist, anti-imperialist worldview captured in the Booker speech itself.

Confrontation and directness, of course, are central to Kelman's art as well as his criticism. In 'Elitism and English Literature, Speaking as a Writer' he insists 'good literature is nothing when it is not being dangerous in some way or another and those in positions of power will always be suspicious of anything that might affect their security.'[8] He adds that 'true literary art makes some folk uncomfortable.' 'Good' and 'true' art is in aggressive battle with power, actively attacking capitalism and imperialism. Artistic method is not separate from this battle. Kelman's descriptions of his own techniques and influences often draw on the language of political subversion, as when he credits the American writer Tillie Olsen with exemplifying 'ways to high-jack third-person narrative from the voice of imperial authority'.[9] Later in the same essay, we hear a combination of the precise, crafted, creative voice found in Kelman's fiction, and the shrill directness of the polemical scrapper:

> Prose fiction was exciting at this level. Somebody was punching fuck out ye but ye went away and attended the cuts, had a shower, and came back with Daddy's axe. Tillie's work was a weapon. The true function of grammar. Make yer point.[10]

This blend of voices underscores a difficulty in Kelman's critical reception. Journalists sent to interview Kelman seem to expect full-throated, barely controlled vitriol, and often confess arriving with a prefabricated image and set of infamous Kelman stories in mind.[11] David Robinson dwells on this anxiety in his *Scotsman* review of *Kieron Smith, boy* ('I've never interviewed Kelman before, and it starts well') and captures, simultaneously, the author's frustration with being interviewed and annoyance at being misunderstood and misrepresented.[12] Undoubtedly, 'awkward Kelman' is a self-perpetuating myth; the more it is recycled by lazy journalists, the more Kelman bridles, cementing the stereotype. But anger and resistance can be valid without being effective. Patrick Doyle, the teacher-agitator of *A Disaffection*, admits 'I have a lot of failures.'

> My failure rate is quite high. I get reminders about it at school. I get subtle tellings off. But I dont care, ha ha ha. Naw but seriously, I dont. I really do not care one way or the other. Ach.[13]

Patrick's 'Ach' suggests otherwise, and the novel ends with him contemplating both flight and suicide, seemingly fleeing the police. Fortunately, James Kelman is made of sturdier stuff than many of his characters. But his insistently oppositional worldview frustrates some of his admirers, and enables detractors to dismiss him out of hand.

Political sympathy has readerly limits. In a review of Kelman's essay collection "*And the Judges Said . . .*", the Marxist critic Terry Eagleton describes Kelman as 'the kind of man whom anyone at the sticky end would want on their side, a writer who combines intense local engagement with generously international perspectives' – before lambasting Kelman's 'swingeing generalisations', 'pathetic clichés', 'truculent self-indulgence' and 'shoot-from-the-hip style'.[14] In his essay 'The Humanist's Dilemma: a polemic against Kelman's polemics,' Alan Freeman notes that Kelman is 'regaled and reviled in equal measure, but on either side, critics confirm the integrity and commitment of his art.'[15] His criticism has often been regarded as a separate matter. Joan McAlpine observes that 'many people confuse the political essayist and activist with the novelist. [Kelman's] fiction is, of course, informed by his world view, but it is never hectoring or judgmental. It is supremely subtle.'[16] In Freeman's view, the reductive, Manichean worldview of oppressors and conspiracies found in Kelman's essays abandons the 'crucial balancing element' found in his fiction, contradicting and perhaps even compromising its humanist vision.[17]

> Where his fiction fuses human worth with individual and local detail, his polemics sweep aside specificity, preclude political or moral nuance, and antagonise the potential force of the aesthetic radicalism that motivates and marks his art. Taken on his own terms, Kelman supplants one corrupt discourse with another, condemning the committed artist to the same ceaseless but futile agitation as the characters he creates.[18]

Freeman suggests that the author's distrust of academia and the literary establishment reflect Kelman's anxieties about his art and voice being co-opted by or constrained within the culture and entertainment industries. Kelman's awkwardness with reviewers is 'a badge, a totem against absorption into the elite'.[19] But it is more than that, also. Freeman sees Kelman's forceful moral clarity, and radical rejection of bourgeois cultural values, as belonging to the Scottish traditions of 'enlightenment communitarianism and Christian socialism'.[20] In order to grasp its complexity and its value, we need to see Kelman's polemical anger and rhetorical stridency in relation to such contexts and sources.

Kelman's longest non-fictional text, 'A Look at Franz Kafka's Three Novels', highlights ethical as well as artistic influences. Begun as an undergraduate dissertation at the University of Strathclyde, the essay also highlights Kelman's talents as a literary analyst. Kelman has recently described the first-person 'I-voice' in fiction as 'the mental masturbation of the bourgeoisie'[21]; the Kafka essay documents the early development of his thinking about the politics of narrative method. Kelman admires the sixteen-year-old Kafka's 'committed socialism' and the Czech writer's attempts to represent the realities of history and capitalism in his fiction in a direct and unmediated way. He notes Kafka's distaste for what he called Dickens's 'rude characterizations', insisting 'Kafka's desire was to create individuals rather than "images"'; above all, he is drawn to Kafka's 'continual battle to submerge interior reflection within the narrative', and the political implications of this technique.[22] In *The Trial*, the reader is given 'a glimpse of the reality' of Joseph K.'s capitalistic and repressive society; in *The Castle*, Kafka perfects the narrative effects of immediacy and directness with the novel's story-within-a-story frame, a technique Kelman describes as solving 'the problem of how to impart historical and other information indirectly, i.e. without having to present it dramatically'.[23]

Parallels with Kelman's own work are obvious. A noteworthy tension in the essay is revealed, however, when Kelman approaches the subject of Kafka's literary reception and canonisation. For Kelman, Kafka's 'place' is in the existential tradition and it is 'a mistake to see his "place" in the modernist tradition'; he later declares 'Marxist critics should simply read the work and find the reality.'[24] There is a sense of impatience with scholarly pigeonholes here, which is understandable enough, but Kelman's discussions of modernism, modernity and 'reality' are too narrowly and fixedly defined. By uncontroversial, broadly historical readings of modernism (the aesthetic movement) and modernity (the socio-historical moment) Kafka can certainly be viewed as a political writer, an existential writer and a modernist; the terms are not mutually exclusive. Perhaps the unique place Kafka holds in Kelman's own identity as a writer makes him impatient of such generalities; it is none the less instructive to examine the modernist context he seeks to displace. A more 'academic' look at politics under modernity is not only a corrective to Kelman's simplified image of Kafka's realist commitment, but illustrates the potential value of the political intellectualism to which Kelman's polemics often seem hostile.

The 'reality' of the ideological formation of contemporary capitalism and 'the modern' is far more dynamic and dialectical than Kelman admits. Modernity's 'reality' is characterised by a dynamic set of forces: turmoil, oppression, destruction, constant renewal, consumption, appropriation, and creation and resistance; modernism's cultural productions are hybrid and multifarious. A view of modernity's dialectical nature can be found in Walter Benjamin's 'Theses on the Philosophy of History' and his magnum opus, *The Arcades Project*. In the latter work's section on nineteenth-century expositions, for example, Benjamin documents a structural and political irony. The economically driven space of the exposition was repressive, spatially and imaginatively organised by colonial, racial and religious codes of superiority and inferiority. The expositions enabled the development of free-trade ideology, were used as showrooms for commodities and armaments, and were aggressively policed; however, that same repressive space of the marketplace was also a fertile laboratory that gave rise to the labour movement and international peace and solidarity organisations.[25]

Despite being very pessimistic about capitalism and commodity culture, Benjamin's dark vision of history and society is tempered by a resigned and matter-of-fact understanding that modernity is characterised by ceaseless battles for justice, creative and cunning attempts to maintain autonomy and freedom, and continual and inescapable compromises. For Benjamin, the nineteenth century is a harbinger of things to come in the twentieth and beyond; his sense of history is empowering without flinching from the actuality of power relations in social life. 'The tradition of the oppressed', for Benjamin, 'teaches us that "the state of emergency" in which we live is not the exception but the rule. We must attain to a conception of history that is in keeping with this insight.'[26] Benjamin is a valuable foil here because his work, like Kelman's, attempts to locate and identify resistant cultural pressures in the midst of rampant exploitation and oppression. Both also share a faith in the radical artist-seer whose work and life are evidence of the fragmentary and difficult, but knowable and accessible signs of autonomy and freedom.

Kelman's work on Scotland's indigenous Common Sense philosophical tradition can be linked to Benjamin's 'modernist' political vision. Benjamin argues that we have organic ways of knowing (what Kelman calls 'forms of natural reason'[27]); in moments of crisis and in the everyday, the realities of capitalism's exploitative nature can be discerned under the surface of things in material reality, and in cities and social spaces, as well. Benjamin makes the provocative suggestion that it is precisely the untrained, organic reader who can read the surface or materiality of history of narrative, while being unaware of the formal and stylistic subtleties that scholarly readers are trained to observe and take note of. When he is not reacting to academic discourses and disciplinary practices, Kelman makes similar points in his discussions of an individual's native reasoning skills and powers of analysis and reflection (for example, in the long essay on Noam Chomsky and its discussion of the Scottish philosophers David Hume and Thomas Reid).[28] His memories of his own adolescent encounters with art, a subject revisited in this chapter's conclusion, also support Benjamin's speculations and his readings of the layered, fluid and multifaceted nature of reality in both modern and contemporary times.

Simon Kövesi importantly notes that Kelman's formative period as a writer was 'concurrent with the height of the British class war', his first two novels appearing at the peak of ideological conflict during the miners' strike of 1984–5.[29] From the start, class has been the dominant political issue in criticism both of, and by, James Kelman. But his essays also reveal debts to and affiliations with politicised Third World cultural activists. Kelman has, for example, been involved in human rights protests alongside Dub poet Linton Kwesi Johnson, whose Dub poetry of the 1980s protests against British racism and the politics of Thatcherism.[30] In his non-fiction works and interviews Kelman has spoken of influences including the Caribbean Artists Movement (CAM), the Trinidadian poet, activist, trade-unionist and independence fighter John La Rose, South African novelist and anti-apartheid activist Alex La Guma, Nigerian authors Amos Tutuola and Ken Saro-Wiwa, Pakistani fiction writer and essayist, Saadat Hasan Manto, playwright and novelist Sam Selvon, and several others (see Chapter 9 for further discussion of these connections).

Kelman's rhetorical forcefulness is partly inspired by the anti-colonial tradition inaugurated by Frantz Fanon. In his 1959 Speech to the Congress of Black Writers and Artists, 'On National Culture', Fanon identifies the shared cultural and psychological fate of colonised peoples, especially in regard to their experience of and depiction in cultural representations. In order to throw off the shackles of interiorised inferiority, the 'native intellectual' (Kelman has used a similar term, 'indigenous intellectual') must engage in a 'muscular' battle to liberate himself.[31] This battle is characterised by three phases. First the native intellectual assimilates the culture of the colonising culture in order to prove self-worth, then he or she is disturbed and attempts to remember or relocate an autonomous or pre-colonised identity. The third, 'fighting' phase sees the native artist and intellectual '[turn] himself into an awakener of the people; hence comes a fighting literature, a revolutionary literature.'[32] The awakened native intellectual and artist feels 'the need to [. . .] compose the sentence which expresses the heart of the people, and then to become the mouthpiece of a new reality in action.'[33] For Fanon, this nationalist phase of anti-colonial redefinition finds even more robust expression beyond the fighting phase, when the anti-imperialist native artist and intellectual envisions the international and communitarian struggles of colonised peoples.

Kelman's non-fiction shows close connections with the anti-imperialist community of artists Fanon's work helped to inspire. In his interview with John La Rose, for example, the two writers discuss topics ranging from the importance of purging from one's mind 'self-deprecatory, self-contemptuous sayings which have been imposed on society', to the necessity of autonomy in the publishing world.[34] Kelman notes that the New Beacon Press enabled La Rose to 'reclaim' the history of Britain's Afro-Caribbean communities and radical history; by contrast, Kelman remarks, Scottish literature is marginalised even in Scottish libraries and bookstores: 'you get these wee sections tucked round a corner, often in quotes – "Scottish" – that's where you find Scottish writing.'[35]

Kelman's complex orientation to Scottish nationalism is strongly influenced by anti-colonial discourse. For Kelman 'Scotland is a "colonised culture" [whose] cultural institutions are controlled by people who "don't really value the Scottish tradition and don't really know it too well".'[36] Kelman has expressed distrust of Scottish nationalism's official political channels, but sympathy for the cause of cultural autonomy. His analysis harks directly back to Fanon; ingrained prejudice against Scottish language means 'children grow up learning they are inferior and their parents are inferior.'[37] Kelman views the 'local' politics of language in Scotland in international terms, gravitating to writers from the former British empire 'because they are used to having English shoved down their throats.'[38] The La Rose interview gives a flavour of the 'generously international perspectives' to which Eagleton referred, and the centrality of language to Kelman's anti-colonial affiliations. The conversation with La Rose moves fluidly from a discussion of both writers' investment in orality (the *kaiso* or calypso tradition and its origins in popular history and protest), the importance of public performance (ranging from theatrical performances to Carnival), to working-class educational activism (the Working Men's Associations). The expansive, free-wheeling discussion uncovers a wide range of intellectual cross-pollinations and transnational alliances, moving easily from Mahatma Gandhi to the Mau Maus, and from Russian writers and musical composers to the struggle to release political prisoners in Kenya. There is a relaxed but morally excited tone to the conversation, quite remote from the rigid certainties of Kelman's rhetoric on the page.

Several of Kelman's essays contain 'interiorised', stream-of-consciousness passages reminiscent of the fiction, some of which are wildly inventive, like 'There Is a First-Order Radical Thinker of European Standing Such That He Exists: or, Tantalising Twinkles', an almost jazz-like improvisational essay on canonical philosophers, the origins of academic and cultural value, and the power of native or indigenous common sense.[39] The essay 'Let the Wind Blow High Let the Wind Blow Low', Kelman's discussion of Scottish voters' political exhaustion and distrust of 'the U.K. political system' after the 1992 General Election in *Some Recent Attacks*, is another example of an essay that successfully integrates rhetorical and artful language, riffs and rants.[40]

In other essays, the attack mode interrupts the engaging stream-of-consciousness narration; for example, in the recent autobiographical 'Afterword' to *An Old Pub Near the Angel*, affecting memories suddenly transform into invective ('The artist must say to the academics, Fight yer own fucking war'[41]). It is worth noting that many of the published essays were first delivered at public speaking events. Kelman often uses the word 'talk' to emphasise the communal nature of the speech, as opposed to the words 'lecture' or even 'speech', both of which imply an academic exercise or a passive reception, rather than a conversation with an audience. In many essays and interviews, Kelman disparages the academic world's discomfort with passion and emotion; in the La Rose interview he remarks, 'That's part of the education system [. . .] You are taught that personal experience and responses are invalid.'[42]

The reader familiar with the affective sympathy found in Kelman's fiction, the intimacy that is forged by the comradely relationship between the 'third-party' narrator and the central protagonist and extended to the reader, is sometimes confronted by a startling difference in his essays: namely, a difference of tactic and style. Urgency and outrage propel the essays directly into the area of struggle, placing the reader in the midst of crisis (even past crisis). 'Shouting at the Edinburgh Fringe Forum' (1987), for example, immediately locates us within a specific and charged political atmosphere. Kelman is tonally direct, employing a broad sarcasm:

> When I speak of the present Government [. . .] not just its Tory Administration, I include Her Majesty's Most Loyal and Trusted Opposition: the Great British Labour Party, the Liberal/SDP Alliance, Plaid Cymru, the Scottish National Party, and so on, they're all fucking in it together.[43]

While the strident voice of the judge rings out from some essays and talks, others reveal the world-weary endurance of the testimonial witness.

The emotionally invested nature of Kelman's political writing is clear in the early 1990s essay 'ATTACK NOT RACIST, say police'. The capitalised title may shout, but the essay is plaintive as well as harrowing in its discussion of widespread racial and ethnic violence in Britain during this period (and some would argue, to date). 'One method of influencing the authorities', Kelman writes, 'lies in presenting the public with the evidence directly.'[44] Accordingly, the reader's own emotional response becomes central to an ethics of witnessing, commemoration and solidarity: 'People find it difficult to cope when they hear about these crimes. Perhaps it is not unnatural that a first response is to turn your mind from the news.'[45] The novelist's art brings vivid depth to the subject; Kelman's own memory of 'being sold raffle tickets' at an anti-racist event by 'two wee girls with big grins, obviously sisters' injects a piercing human reality to a necessarily discursive and at times technical exposition of police complacency, state legal evasion and media complicity. The smiling girls are the daughters of the mini-cab driver Kuldip Singh Sekhon, murdered at work in 1989 by a 'known racist' with a previous conviction for assaulting an Asian man, who 'either forgot or did not have time to rob the victim he managed to stab approximately fifty-eight times.'[46] This stark, unsentimental, unshockable voice – a 'realist' voice for stating and facing horrific facts – is a strong feature of Kelman's political writing. 'In his final summing up' at the trial of Sekhon's assailant, Kelman records, 'the judge declared: "I would say there is no evidence that this was a racist attack".'[47]

> Yet none should be too surprised; we all know that racist abuse and violation, including murder, are the experience of the various non-European communities from John O'Groats to Land's End. This sort of incident is not untypical [. . .] given that the British State is itself racist, people should not act as though it is some sort of social phenomenon, an aberration. But most people do not act after that fashion.[48]

Immediacy and passion are central to Kelman's political essays, but aspects of his style attempt to convert vehemence into rational argument.

Documenting injustice and *forcefully disrupting* the reader's (listener's) comfortable distance from actual violence are Kelman's goals as a speaker-essayist. His arresting prose grabs us by the lapels and brings us into direct contact with scenes of crime, corruption, oppression and cowardice. But the sheer force of this style engenders a rhetorical problem. Kelman's essays share his fiction's 'passion for proximity', and intense focus on concrete reality.[49] But analytical reasoning and critical distance are depicted as bourgeois postures and sterile academic practices, especially discrediting in the face of systemic violence and oppression.[50] Confrontation with factual reality is often privileged over nuanced discussion or analysis. Partly, this reflects Kelman's realistic expectation of what campaigning prose can achieve. 'Most campaigns fail' he readily admits; 'but what does it mean to win?'

> All campaigns concern miscarriages of justice in one sense or another. They can
> involve the worst sorts of brutality. In many instances 'to win' a campaign is
> simply to have acknowledged by those in authority that a miscarriage of justice
> has occurred.[51]

Simply establishing the *fact* of oppression, forcing recognition of its reality, is
an important goal of this writing. But this emphasis does not fully explain the
difference in temperament between Kelman's fiction and essays. The 'openness' of Kelman's fiction is matched by the 'closed' ideological certainties of
the activist; Joan McAlpine notes that 'Kelman's political certainty stands
in stark contrast to his alienated, often insecure, characters, who struggle
to make sense of the world around them.'[52] Take Kelman's novel *Translated
Accounts*, which places the reader in painfully immediate contact with narratives of incomprehensible and nearly unspeakable violence. The difficulty
and uncertainty of deciphering the 'accounts' is surely part of the ethical
engagement the novel demands: imaginative sympathy *despite* the opacity of
the real, and the absence of sure facts.

The result of Kelman's aggressive oppositional stance in his non-fiction
writing is that many of the essays effect a kind of *affective dissonance*; the just
causes being addressed in the talks reveal the stark forces of actual forms of
repression and exploitation (racial violence, police brutality, callous disre-
gard for workers' health and rights, ethnic and sectarian hatred[53]), but the
speaker's righteous anger often inflicts a violence of its own. This may be
intentional – Kelman describes the 'authentic' artist's language as a weapon,
an axe – a tool with which to resist the 'reverberating assembly line of cutting
tools and hammers' used on the 'Others' by the powers that be.[54] The Tom
Leonard poem, 'A Short History of the British Judiciary', from which "*And
the Judges Said . . .*" takes its title, reflects this 'us and them' worldview and
pinpoints a contradiction in the voice of the essays: 'And their judges spoke
with one dialect, / but the condemned spoke with many voices.'[55]

In his fiction, Kelman's technique of 'submerg[ing] interior reflection
within the narrative' creates an intimacy and potentially a fidelity between
character and narrator, immersing the reader in the character's consciousness and social situation. In *How late it was, how late* or *Kieron Smith, boy*, the
reader becomes the narrator's observant mate and character's guardian angel.
Kelman's definition of solidarity ('a mixture of sympathy and empathy'[56])
is embodied by narrative method in the fiction; in the essays, the reader is
placed squarely on to the battlefield of language, power and politics, and is
sometimes directly in the line of fire. The judge's voice is Kelman's; if the
reader is on the 'wrong side', well, solidarity be damned. H. Gustav Klaus
notes that Kelman's rhetorical tone in the essays is that of a 'judge of judges,
a fearless adjudicator'; he observes that the author defends civic rights in as

spirited a manner as he attacks the powerful.[57] But the fixed worldview of the all-knowing 'judge of judges', with its admitted class resentments and Manichean view of committed artists and activists in opposition to the self-deluded assimilationists, 'huffy academics' and sell-outs, also severely flattens the world and its social and political complexities, and diminishes the powerfully affective humanist ethos that is evident in Kelman's fiction and his well-documented *lived* political commitments.[58] The polemical essays rarely acknowledge that most human beings speak with many voices.

A person can acknowledge the world's power structures, oppressive policies and exploitative economic realities without succumbing to a rigidly codified world of heroic working-class and revolutionary figures on one hand, and co-opted middle-class evil-doers entirely beholden to the corrupt institutions in which they live and work. For this critic Kelman's representations of the academic world are semi-familiar (its traditionalism and disciplinary training methods) and distressingly caricatured. Seldom is there an acknowledgement of the 'committed', 'authentic' or 'engaged' work – his adjectives for heroic or comradely artists – that is taking place in the scholarly world, and not just by leftists. Teaching itself is committed work. Academics and the Humanities in general have been under attack from corporatist forces and right-wing critics since the 1980s, from the latter in ways reminiscent of the 1950s Red Scare. Corporatists focus on the production of useful, business and industry-oriented knowledge that will reap profits and serve the marketplace, a view that Kelman condemns and broadly projects on to academia. Publicly funded universities are particularly vulnerable to these increasingly popular privatisation schemes.

In 'Artists and Value', an essay written for a talk at the Glasgow School of Art in 1989-90, Kelman confidently discusses how clichés, stereotypes, and generalisations represent lazy thinking and create 'bad' art; conventional and formulaic ways of looking and thinking are the source of the problem.[59] While Kelman does not consider his own political views synonymous with what he is describing as dominant culture's mainstream ideology, there is a relationship between formulaic perceptions and beliefs and ideological sectarianism; both fail to be persuasive and inscribe an inflexible, unchanging and unchangeable, doctrinaire worldview.

In Kelman's most recent work, the judge's voice is melded with that of the socialist and popular historian. Kelman has throughout his career been concerned with what Howard Zinn calls 'a people's history'; Kelman has frequently bemoaned the erasure or invisibility of British working-class and racial and ethnic communities' histories. Recent non-fiction also highlights Kelman's gifts as a memoirist and storyteller, glimpses of which can be found in "And the judges said . . .". For example, 'When I Was That Age Did Art Exist?', the two talks delivered to students at Dallas's Highland Park High

School in 1991, foreshadow Kelman's novel *Kieron Smith, boy;*[60] they also
directly address sexual abuse and the omnipresence of bullies in the world,
subjects avoided or mentioned only obliquely in adults' conversations with
teenagers. In a few short pages, he incorporates concerns that are evident in
the entire corpus of his critical work: the exploitation of workers and their
labour (sweatshops and children's lives elsewhere); minority and working-
class people's socially inscribed and internalised feelings of inferiority; the
difficult and necessary process of finding one's own voice; the legitimacy of
rebellion; and the necessity of art in life and the world.[61]

The biographical 'Afterword' from the reissued *An Old Pub Near the Angel*
and the exhaustive 'Introduction' to the Socialist activist Hugh Savage's
memoir, *Born Up a Close*, both continue in this combined autobiographical-
historical vein. These two essays might be the ideal places for the un-initiated
Kelman reader to begin to familiarise himself or herself; the essays might
also enable the Kelman-weary reader to revisit the author's work. Both
pieces span the author's life and work, and powerfully represent his engagement with people, politics, and the local and wider worlds. Kelman is doing
for Scotland's working-class communities what the recently opened Black
Cultural Archives in Brixton is doing for London's Afro-Caribbean communities: voicing the people's stories and documenting how they worked,
struggled, lived and played. The introduction to *Born Up a Close* opens with
a story about Kelman and Savage's initial meeting during the tumultuous
Glaswegian City of Culture year in 1990, moves on to an important discussion of 'indigenous history' and philosophy, and includes the 'spectacular'
socialist history of the 1920s and the Irish Home Rule and Fenian Republican
movements, including local, Glaswegian Bloody Friday (1919) demonstra-
tions. The essay concludes with a charming story about Savage's 'massive'
dog, Rory the Rotweiler.

Both essays capture the essence of the James Kelman whom I know and
greatly admire; they also expand upon Kelman's earlier essay on the continuing legacy and influence of the Scottish Common Sense philosophical
tradition, historical scholarship that Kelman began in 1988, and a philosophical practice that is visible in the talk to the Dallas high-school students.[62]
Kelman's most recent essays, including some directly autobiographical journalistic pieces,[63] highlight what Benjamin saw and what Kelman's own work
makes evident, beyond the anger – that in the midst of capitalism and com-
merce, even during periods of brutal repression, resonant expression inspires,
and the currency of ideas flows and is indefatigable.[64]

CHAPTER SIX

Kelman's Drama

David Archibald

I enjoy working in drama – stage, radio, television, film – but it very rarely happens; all these other people come between yourself and the piece. And I'm not talking about actors here, but the sorts of pressure that gets applied to directors, producers and theatres. The work gets squeezed to the point where it hurts to continue. The most obvious example is language itself, if you want to work in drama, and create it from your own experience, if that experience happens to be male working class culture around west central Scotland. Be prepared to censor and suppress your characters, or write only from tiny corners of that experience. In prose fiction the freedom to work honestly exists, although you may have to fight for it. In those other areas of literature, I mean drama, there is only silence. That sort of aesthetic integrity does not exist in radio and television, and seldom on film.

James Kelman[1]

James Kelman's reputation as one of Scotland's finest living authors is based largely on his prose fiction. Yet, in a period spanning over three decades, Kelman has also produced a considerable dramatic *oeuvre*, although, unfortunately, much of this work has never been published or performed. This chapter provides a short overview of Kelman's writing for radio, screen and stage and, in the process, charts a move from the image of Kelman as a private, fiercely autonomous author, to a more public figure, entangled (not always successfully) in the collaborative process.

We might begin by outlining Kelman's dramatic output.[2] Three stage plays have been published: *The Busker* (1985), *In the Night* (1987) and *Hardie and Baird: The Last Days* (1990).[3] Three further plays were performed by Arches Theatre in Glasgow – *One, Two – Hey!* (1994), *Herbal Remedies* and *They Make These Noises*[4] (both 2007) – as well as a short monologue, *Man to Man*, which was performed in the venue's toilets as part of the company's 'Spend a Penny' season (2007).[5] Five further stage plays have never been performed: *Big Star, Redemption, Refugees, The Soup Enigma* and *The Spanner in the Works*. Work produced on radio includes an earlier version of *Hardie and Baird: The Last Days* (BBC Radio Scotland, 1978) and an earlier version of *The Soup*

Enigma entitled *The Art of the Big Bass Drum* (BBC Radio 3, 1988).[6] A translated version of Kelman's own adaptation of *How late it was, how late* was
broadcast on German radio in 2005, and the Texas-based theatre company,
Rude Mechanicals, performed a stage version, adapted by the company,
in 2003. Radio versions of *The Busker* and *In the Night* have been written,
although not yet performed, and two further radio plays, *In With the Doctor*
and *He Knew Him Well*, have never been performed on radio.[7]

Kelman has also written a number of film scripts – two short screenplays,
Unlucky and *The Hitchhiker*, screen versions of *The Busconductor Hines* and *A
Situation*, and an original screenplay, *A Young Man's Story* – although none of
this work has been filmed.[8] Kelman's absence from the screen may be about
to change, however, as Scottish Screen recently (March 2009) announced
Content Development Funding of £18,750 for *Dirt Road to Lafayette*, which
Kelman describes as 'an original screenplay based in [the] US southern states,
about a young male accordion player who goes on a three week holiday with
his dad to stay with relations in northern Alabama; music is crucial within
it – accordion based Cajun/Zydeco, Conhunto, Newfie and Scots-Irish.'[9] The
film is set to be directed by Kenny Glenaan.[10] In total, there are twenty-one
separate texts, of which eleven were developed out of, or are adaptations
or versions of, Kelman's prose writing.[11] In addition, sections of *Translated
Accounts* were narrated as part of a stage production, *Lives Were Around Me*,
by Battery Opera in Vancouver in 2009.

Simon Kövesi suggests that 'class, politics, language and masculinity'
are the central, and connected, themes running through Kelman's work.[12]
Certainly, all four themes are present in Kelman's most established dramatic
piece, *Hardie and Baird: The Last Days*. Set in the aftermath of what has
become known as the Scottish Insurrection or Radical War of 1820, *Hardie
and Baird* is a dramatic rendering of the final days of two of the movement's
leaders, John Baird and Andrew Hardie, as they await execution for their
role in the failed rebellion.[13] In the opening prologue the narrator states,
'never, never, shall they be forgot', yet, as Kelman has noted elsewhere, 'this
part of Scottish history is more or less unknown; no such radical aspect of
Scottish history is taught our children in our schools.'[14] *Hardie and Baird* sits
comfortably alongside the 'history from below' school of historiography that
gained momentum in the 1960s and 1970s and which constructed historical
narratives based on the lives of workers and peasants rather than the lives
of Kings and Queens. When rulers do get a mention in *Hardie and Baird*
it is in far from positive terms; speaking of the British Army, Baird states,
'for the past twenty year we've been destroying liberty wherever we find
it, right across Europe – Italy, France, Germany, Spain – sticking tyrants
into power.'[15] *Hardie and Baird* can be placed alongside the rich tradition of
Scottish radical theatre of the 1970s, exemplified by the work of the 7:84

(Scotland) group, but it is no simple polemic and is far from didactic. The two Radicals exemplify differing worldviews; while Baird draws back from the religious dignitaries who visit the pair in prison, Hardie embraces them. Hardie, moreover, suggests that life has meaning only through religion: 'It's only through him we see it isni all a waste of time. All this world Johnnie it's nothing, just a cheat; born out of sin and in sin till it comes to God.'[16] Baird, on the other hand, seems committed to an engagement in class struggle as a way of giving meaning to his life: 'They've never gave us nothing wioot it being wrested from them, never. We've aye had to fight. Every bit o progress, it's had to get tore aff them, they'd have gave us nothing if we'd left it to them – nothing.'[17]

Struggles over history and memory are given a more modern and abstract twist in *In the Night*. As three officials interrogate a man and woman in their own home about their left-wing activities, one of the officials states 'There isnt any history. Nothing has happened in the past. Nothing. They admit of nothing at all. They say that there isnt any, that it doesnt exist; they say that it simply doesnt exist. They say that history does not exist.'[18] The official's words, which resonate with contemporary debates about the philosophy of history – specifically, the famous 'End of History' prognosis of Francis Fukuyama – also conjure up a vision of authoritarian figures who wield control over both present and past. *In the Night* creates a chilling power dynamic, the absurdity of the situation and the stylised sparseness of the language recalling the plays of Harold Pinter.[19]

The third play in the published collection, *The Busker*, was written for Kelman's friend, the Glasgow actor and musician Alan Tall. In this three-hander, in three short acts, the eponymous 'Busker' tries to earn some money while 'Ponce' attempts to muscle in on the action. Male characters predominate in Kelman's plays, but when women do appear they are often central to the drama. Here the conflict between the two characters is interrupted with the appearance of 'Lady', with whom they both aspire to connect. *The Busker* is indicative of Kelman's interest in music, which is also evident in *One, Two – Hey!* and in its companion piece, *Redemption*. Both plays were inspired by the Blues Poets, a blues band who played regular sessions in the 1980s and 1990s in the Scotia Bar, a Glasgow pub that was associated with the Workers' City project in 1990.[20] All three plays have Glaswegian characters, but the music reflects Scottish working-class connections with US popular culture: the use of Bob Dylan in *The Busker*; the repertoire of what the author describes as 'classic rock/pop/soul/blues' songs in *One, Two – Hey!*, and the inclusion of Hank Williams tracks and the theme tune from the US television western, *Bonanza*, in *Redemption*. 'Musical Theatre' might not be the term one might expect to associate with Kelman, but in formal terms, at least, both *One, Two – Hey!* and *Redemption* fit comfortably under that heading.

In relation to language, Kövesi suggests

> Kelman's fictional texts are not voiced in standard English, or in standard Scots: occasionally pockmarked by quasi-phonetic rendition, and linguistic markers of locality – always of Glasgow where recognisable – the voices are broadly variable, polyvalent, inconsistent, and rendered in fluid, changing Kelmanese, a style all of his own making. There is nothing pure about his language other than its consistent idiosyncrasy.[21]

The language in Kelman's drama is often characterised by the specific rootedness of his native city. Most of the plays are set in Glasgow or have Glaswegian characters, but locality is not fetishised. For example, in his unpublished notes on *Redemption*, Kelman writes 'I have written it for Glasgow-speaking voices and much of the humour seems to derive from the language but I am interested to know if anyone thinks it can be played in other voices.'[22] In his published notes on *The Busker* he suggests that 'this play is written for actors at home with the Glasgow accent; but they should not feel constrained by the words on the page.'[23] In Kelman's later, unpublished notes on the play, it becomes clear that linguistic *contrasts* take priority:

> I see that this play could work with three people from a different background and the location could shift. It could be three Dubliners in Manchester. Is there any equivalent in your country? Could it be three people from Lubbock landing in Dallas? Could it be three people from the Bronx in Austin, in San Francisco? Texans in NY? Would the language subtlety work? I don't know.[24]

H. Gustav Klaus notes that Kelman's narratives 'do not rely on plot, incident or conflict. Instead of elaborate lifelines, they present glimpses or fragments of ordinary, mostly uneventful, certainly unspectacular lives.'[25] In a 1989 interview Kelman outlines his thinking about the absence of conventional 'plot' in his work:

> You don't need a beginning, middle and end at all [. . .] There's no need to be saying or thinking 'When's the murder or bank robbery going to happen?'. No such abnormal event will occur – the kind of event that seems to motivate almost all mainstream fiction whether in book or screen form. In reality these events are abnormal.[26]

Kelman's drama, like his prose, refuses to observe classic Aristotelian form (e.g. 'unity' of action, place and time). On the contrary, Kelman adopts a more experimental, modernist theatrical style and his dramatic work is marked by studies into character rather than being driven by action. This unwillingness to over-dramatise his work is apparent in the endings to the plays, which often conclude *media res*, or refuse dramatic conclusion. For instance, the final words of Andrew Hardie, as he stood awaiting execution on the gallows, were 'I die a martyr to the cause of truth and justice.'[27] It is a speech full of theatrical potential, yet Kelman opts to exclude this, ending the play with the two condemned men preparing to sleep on the night before their execution. His open-ended conclusion allows the audience the opportunity to relate to the characters on a familiar, 'ordinary' scale, and also allows greater scope for the audience to construct meaning from the play, rather than slavishly following plot and narrative.

When reading all of Kelman's plays together it becomes apparent that he is a writer with a strong, overall artistic vision for the production. This is, on occasion, exemplified by his stage directions. In *Hardie and Baird*, for instance, he writes, '**Lord President** enters. He walks to centrestage and stands downstage from **Hardie** and **Baird**, but not as far as the **Two Soldiers**.'[28] The specificity of the arrangements of the actors on stage, which would generally be categorised as 'blocking' and regarded as the work of a play's director, perhaps reflects a tension between Kelman as prose writer – in complete control of his output – and Kelman as collaborator, forced to work with other artistic participants.[29] In a 1994 interview, Kelman highlights the collective nature of the dramatic process when he states,

> I do see drama as a separate medium. I don't see it as being something where every comma is mine, in the way that I would with a short story. It was written in the awareness that this is a team effort. There's a squad involved in this and things can happen that will be exciting and surprise me.[30]

Yet, a possible further example of this tension is evident in the introduction to *Hardie and Baird* where Kelman states, 'I had worked with Ian Brown [the play's director] before and respected his wish to *know* a text rather than *interpret* it' (emphasis added).[31] This distinction seems to signal Kelman's resistance to the dominant trend in modern literary theory, and in contemporary theatre, which moves away from the notion of a work having a singular, knowable meaning, and relishes the idea of texts being open to various interpretations (or to *being* only interpretation). The strong consensus in favour of this shift has practical implications. Not only are writers more willing to allow directors to interpret their work; directors are less keen to work with writers who have (and enforce) a singular view of their work. In this respect, Kelman may be out of step with the current theatrical orthodoxy. We can only speculate, but this tension may be a contributing factor in the difficulty his recent dramatic work has faced in reaching the stage.

Drama is certainly a different beast from prose fiction. Working with actors, directors, designers and so on involves not only collaboration, but often compromise too. Moreover, labour-intensive art forms such as theatre often require direct state funding, or at the least the involvement of state-subsidised theatres and, therefore, contact with an arts bureaucracy.[32] In an interview in 1999, Kelman outlined some of the difficulties that can arise in this process. After refusing to submit his work to the 'literature committee' of the Traverse Theatre in Edinburgh he stated, 'I still can't get a play done at a place like The Traverse without doing a clown routine for the bastards [. . .] These theatres are theirs, they belong to the admin officers, they've got nothing to do with us, the artists.'[33] Kövesi captures the strength, but also hints at the potential cost, of Kelman's abhorrence for bureaucratic assessment:

> For committed and consistent political reasons, Kelman will not submit to expectations and institutional requirements, even and especially when being paid, even when it would be easier, would be politically correct, personally polite and strategically efficacious for his various projects, to keep quiet.[34]

There are, therefore, a number of factors that might help explain the lack of Kelman's work on radio, screen and stage, yet when his work does receive an airing, the results are positive.

This is evidenced by the response to Kelman's work when it is produced on the Scottish stage. His most recent contribution was a double-bill comprising *They Make These Noises* and *Herbal Remedies*, which both played to sell-out audiences with the latter, in particular, receiving strong notices from critics. *Herbal Remedies* opens with two male down-and-outs. One, 'Mate', is bare-foot; the other, 'Crutch', is one-legged. The characters wait while a woman, Clarissa, sleeps off a hangover on a nearby bench. The play carries echoes of some of the seminal works of twentieth-century drama: the dialogue of Harold Pinter's *The Caretaker*, the park bench setting which is central to Edward Albee's *Zoo Story*, and both the characters and the leafless tree (placed centre-stage), which invite parallels with Samuel Beckett's *Waiting for Godot*. Kelman has long been associated with, or at least been criticised for, what has been termed 'miserabilism'.[35] If that charge is inappropriate for his prose fiction, it is equally misplaced with reference to his dramatic writing, which is laced with dark humour. Writing in *The Scotsman*, Joyce McMillan describes the play as 'a chunk of Kelman as hilarious as a piece of vintage Frankie Howerd'.[36] Mark Brown in The *Daily Telegraph* wrote that it was 'often hilarious'.[37] Of the play overall, however, Brown argues that 'it lacks the universal reach of Beckett, and is very much a play of momentary pleasures.' Kelman's fiction clearly influences his reception as a dramatist. In *The Guardian*, Mark Fisher laments 'what a shame that a novelist with such an acute ear for the patterns of colloquial speech should have been absent from the theatre for so long.' His mixed review goes on, however, to suggest that the play is short on 'dramatic weight' and is 'not a major play'.[38] David Pollock in the *Financial Times* takes a more positive view, commenting that 'the Arches' publicity boast that Kelman may bear comparison to Beckett or Pinter isn't so far-fetched – he tells a superficially incidental story, yet manages to invest his perfectly pitched and often hilarious lines with a weight of meaning.'[39] The most supportive review, however, comes from McMillan, Scotland's pre-eminent theatre critic: '*Herbal Remedies*', she writes, 'achieves a theatrical lightness of being that belongs only to the greatest drama, a rare sense of sheer pleasure in the joyful play of impulses and ideas in front of an audience' which, in her words, 'confirms Kelman as a writer of huge theatrical gifts.'[40]

To conclude, Kelman's output suggests that he is not a dramatist with a singular style, but one who can move across a wide range of genres, from historical plays (*Hardie and Baird*) to musical theatre (*One, Two – Hey!*, *Redemption*) to work in a register that is more abstract and absurd (*In the Night, Herbal Remedies*), and one who has proven quietly successful at adapting his work across media even if that work has not been performed as often as it merits. That Kelman's work is being adapted and produced in the US and Canada is testimony to the international appeal of his writing; whether audiences closer to his native city will have a greater opportunity to see his work on stage, radio, television or silver screen in the coming years remains to be seen.

II

Critical Contexts

CHAPTER SEVEN

Kelman's Glasgow Sentence

Cairns Craig

Despite having lived for a time in Los Angeles, when his family emigrated to the United States, and despite having lived in London and Manchester, Kelman's art was committed to Glasgow: 'I am always from Glasgow and I speak English always / Always with this Glasgow accent,' he declared.[1] Glasgow represented a boundary – 'I had as a project to write a group of stories set wholly in Glasgow'[2] – which so decisively framed his writing that some of his characters find it impossible to pass beyond the boundary of the city, while others succeed in escaping from Glasgow only by escaping out of Kelman's writing: 'and that was him, out of sight'.[3]

The Glasgow which Kelman's characters inhabit may be the geographical city on the Clyde but it is given very little physical specification. There are no panoramas of tenement rooftops and shipyard gantries such as one finds in earlier Glasgow writing, like George Blake's *The Shipbuilders* (1935); nor does Kelman give the kind of detailed texture of the urban environment that one finds, for instance, in Alasdair Gray's *Lanark* (1981), which describes how its central character 'lived in the middle storey of a corporation tenement that was red sandstone in front and brick behind. The tenement backs enclosed a grassy area divided into greens by spiked railings, and each green had a midden.'[4] In Kelman's writing such physical environments are viewed only through the lens of the character's psyche:

> This rectangle is formed by the backsides of the buildings – in fact it's maybe even a square. A square: 4 sides of equal length and each 2 lines being angled onto each other at 90°. Okay now: this backcourt a square and for each unit of dwellers up each tenement close there exists the ⅓ midden being equal to 2 dustbins [. . .] But then you've got the prowlers coming round when every cunt's asleep. They go exchanging holey dustbins for nice new yins. Holey dustbins: the bottom only portionally there so the rubbish remains on the ground when said dustbins are being uplifted. What a bastard.[5]

What we 'see' as readers is not the backcourt but Hines's incessant effort to reduce the world to orderly mathematical relations; what we are aware of are not the social problems of communal living spaces but the disjunctions in the language through which Hines responds to those spaces, the high-flown rhetoric of 'the bottom only portionally there' disruptively conjoined with the demotic of 'when every cunt's asleep'. Glasgow in Kelman's writing is defined not by the physical spaces that separate the working classes from the middle classes (though this is the source of conflict between Hines and his wife) but the linguistic spaces and verbal territories whose encoding of social hierarchy is replicated in the traditional structure of the novel:

> In prose fiction I saw the distinction between dialogue and narrative as a sum-mation of the political system; it was simply another method of exclusion, of marginalising and disenfranchising different peoples, cultures and communities. I was uncomfortable with 'working-class' authors who allowed 'the voice' of higher authority to control narrative, the place where the psychological drama occurred. How could I write from within my own place and time if I was forced to adopt the 'received' language of the ruling class?[6]

The accepted rules of language are identical with the rule of a particular class and, as a working-class writer, Kelman was determined to overthrow the restrictions which those rules were designed to impose on him:

> Go and write any story at all, providing of course you stay within the bounds, not the bounds of decency or propriety or anything tangible; because that is not the way it works. Nobody issues such instructions. It is all carried out by a series of nudges and winks and tacit agreements. What it amounts to is: go and write a story about a bunch of guys who stand talking in a pub all day but if you have them talking then do not have them talking the language they talk.
>   Pardon?
>   Write a story wherein people are talking, but not talking the language they talk.[7]

Since it cannot have its characters 'talking the language they talk', conven-tional literary realism defeats its own end; what it purveys is an illusion in which everyday reality is rendered both inaudible and invisible. Kelman's writing, on the other hand, takes seriously what many branches of modern linguistics have sought to prove: namely, that the very nature of the world we experience is a function of the language we use, and that it is only in and through an understanding of the workings of language that we can under-stand the 'reality' of the world we inhabit.

To understand the force of this, it is useful to compare Kelman with a writer to whom he is often assumed to be indebted – Tom Leonard, whose exploration of the disjunction between the sound of Glasgow vernacular and the possible ways of representing it in written form was to be one of the major features of experimental Scottish writing in the 1970s (though Kelman himself denies knowing, or being influenced by, Leonard's *Six Glasgow Poems* of 1969).[8] Leonard's was a poetry committed to a 'revolution of the word' that would displace standard English; thus the Biblical formulation, 'In the beginning was the word,' becomes, by a series of transformations, 'nthibegin-ninwuzthiwurd,' because the truth is that 'in the beginning was the sound'.[9] Despite his phonetic rendering of vernacular speech, it was not with 'sound' that Kelman was primarily concerned but with the structure of the sentence. Working-class writers, he argued, had to resist any style that might 'assimilate that conventional grammar'.[10] Instead, they had to study 'the true function of grammar' in order to liberate both writer and character from the constrictions of traditional narrative: 'Go for richness, sophistication, infinite possibility: use the past tense properly, discover its subtlety. Learn yer fucking grammar! Do not be lazy! How does the verb operate in other language cultures?'[11] The mimesis of 'real' language – the language of 'a bunch of guys who stand talking in a pub all day' – was one way of fulfilling the demands of a certain kind of 'realism' but the more effective way of 'breaching linguistic and social taboos', and the artistically effective way of representing 'that self-contained Glasgow' was at the structural level, the level that connected the 'grammar' of narrative to how verbs might 'operate in other language cultures'.[12] Kelman's is an art dedicated to exploring the 'richness' and 'sophistication' of the grammar unique to each of his protagonists.

In this, Kelman was exploiting what he later identified with the linguistics of American theorist Noam Chomsky, to whose anarchist politics Kelman was also attracted. For Chomsky, the powers of language acquisition which every normal human child displays point to the fact that language is a fundamental structure of the human mind, or brain – in all likelihood, *the* fundamental structure. And yet, from this shared underlying structure, each individual is able to develop a language which displays not only the unique features of particular dialects – and Chomsky is insistent that every speaker of English is a speaker of a *dialect* of English – but unique features which also 'distinguish [the speaker's] grammar from that of the speech communities in which he lives'.[13] Chomsky's theory emphasises the fact that human beings inherit rather than acquire language; he believes, as Kelman puts it, in 'forms of knowledge available to people outwith any experience they may have gained from being in the world.'[14] Language is both the product of a set of universal structures which determine consciousness in advance of any experience, and, at the same time, is capable of producing 'new linguistic forms – often new in one's experience or even in the history of the language – and there are no limits to such innovation.'[15] It is only on the basis of this rule-bound, predetermined capacity that language can be 'so rich and sophisticated, capable of such infinite possibility'.[16] The predetermined is thus, however paradoxically, the basis of an infinite freedom, and also the basis of democracy, since all human minds share in 'a fixed framework that is characteristic of the species'[17] and are, therefore, in principle, equal:

> it is fair to say that it is the humanistic conception of man that is advanced and given substance as we discover the rich systems of invariant structures and principles that underlie the most ordinary and humble of human accomplishments.[18]

Even although such 'arguments from human nature and fixed principles are usually regarded as reactionary by the orthodox left', they are, to Kelman, the very foundation of humanity's 'freedom' and its 'inalienable right' 'to not be colonised in any way whatsoever'.[19]

Whereas Chomsky used his theory to search for the common 'deep' structures which underlay all ordinary sentences in particular languages, a 'universal' grammar of the mind, Kelman went in the opposite direction – to explore the individualities of syntax that express the ways in which each of us relates to the world. Dialect, in this sense, is the place of the maximum of linguistic freedom, the maximum assertion of individuality; it is the liberated, anarchic complement of the predetermined, fixed rules from which all language is generated. Kelman's characters are at once an experiment in the freedom to shape sentences in a uniquely individual fashion and, at the same time, an examination of how each of us is sentenced to experiencing a world made possible by the structures of our language. That double perspective could only be achieved by finding a radically new way of shaping the narrative possibilities of the novel; first-person narratives were inadequate to Kelman's purpose because 'when there is no continuity in the writing the perspective of the central character shifts. It starts to feel like a different person.'[20] At the same time, he could not commit to a traditional third-person narrative because that would inevitably invoke a standard by which working-class characters would be condemned as inarticulately sunk in 'the language of the gutter'.[21] The answer – an answer as radical for its time as Joyce's experiments with 'stream of consciousness' in the 1910s – lay in adopting a third-person mode of narration which was not allowed to go beyond the linguistic boundaries of what would have been a first-person narrative. Kelman revised early modernism's 'stream-of-consciousness' revolution to produce a new 'first- and third-person' narrative in which the narrator is under sentence to the character's language rather than the character sentenced by the narrator's.

Kelman's first two novels explore the tension between the predetermination and the freedom of language in contrasting ways. In *A Chancer* (1985), which had largely been written before his first published novel, *The Busconductor Hines* (1984), Kelman adopts a third-person narrative voice which is entirely limited to the perspective of Tammas, the novel's central character, a perspective which might have been rendered through a first-person stream of consciousness technique. Kelman, however, reverses the underlying principle of stream of consciousness by refusing to represent the inner workings of his character's mind, giving the reader no more access to the character's thoughts than any human being has to the thoughts of any other person. This 'third-party narrator' is the very opposite of omniscient, and can therefore provide no explanations for Tammas's actions:

> Naw it's alright. Robert had raised his hand and he smiled. I want to hear about the people that give away their money.
> I'm talking about auld Phil over the road in the betting shop. He doesnt have to work in there you know he just likes to do it, to keep in touch with the game.
> O, I see.
> Aye, he doesnt need to work.
> Mm, just like you . . . Robert frowned and he shifted round on his seat to be facing away from him. Away and grow up son.
> I might and I might no – have to watch it in case I turn out like you.
> Tammas! Margaret was staring at him.
> Robert held his hand up to her. It's alright Margaret . . . He glanced at Tammas: I've got one thing to say to you: why dont you pack your bags and go. The trouble is you *have* grown up, you *are* a big boy. You just dont act like one. And I think it'd be best if you went, and I mean that.
> Aye. Dont worry about it. Tammas was getting onto his feet, gathering his cup and plate and the cigarettes and matches. Soon as the time comes I'll be off, away, dont worry about that. He was at the door and he paused to add, Goodnight folks, pleasant dreams.[22]

The traditional role of the narrator in explaining psychological motivation has disappeared; we are given only the audible, visible and occasionally tactile events in the world, without the markers (inverted commas and so on) that normally separate them in a novel. This radical reduction in the role of the narrator is matched by minimal sentence structures: 'Robert had raised his hand and he smiled.' 'And' is the only possible connector in a world reduced to successive events whose causes in the inner life of the characters are unobservable.

Yet this passage also shows Kelman adopting syntactic features which are not usual in standard English. What might normally have been rendered by 'to face away from him' is replaced by 'he shifted round on his seat *to be* facing away from him,' a locution which adopts the typical preference in Glasgow speech for continuous tenses, a feature echoed in 'Tammas *was getting* on to his feet' (rather than 'got to his feet').[23] Such locutions come close to present-ing not just the character's action but his intention. Robert is not just 'facing away' but is determined 'to be facing away'; Tammas is not just 'getting to his feet' but wants to be seen to be 'getting on to his feet', as though the action is also a statement. In such sentences it is as though a vernacular locution syntactically implies the state of consciousness of the character. In the opposing attitudes of Robert and Thomas we are presented with two radically different responses to the nature of the world. Robert sees himself living in a world of cause and effect where the accumulating weight of the past shapes the nature of the present; people who are grown up should be able to connect their past to their future. For Tammas, however, events do not accumulate towards a conclusion but simply await a certain temporal coincidence: 'Soon as the time comes I'll be off.' Tammas is a 'chancer' – 'Milly doesnt think I should be seeing you. She says you're a chancer'[24] – because he refuses the world of social causality that predefines identity – 'have to watch in case I turn out like you' – and opts for the chance of freedom, which, in his social world, can only be the freedom of chance, a chance symbolised in his obsessive gambling. Kelman's narrative technique thus colludes with Tammas's own refusal to explain himself to anyone, defeating the psychological causality which the traditional structures of the novel have been designed to help us comprehend, but thereby also defeating the assumption that we are each as knowable as characters in a novel. By refusing to allow his novel to *explain* his character's actions, by leaving him (apparently) free to experience the indeterminacies of chance, Kelman reverses authorial domination over a predetermined puppet-character. When Tammas disappears at the novel's conclusion, having accepted the chance of a hitchhike to London, the character (as human being living in Glasgow) escapes the city; the character (as a fiction produced by the language James Kelman has constructed for him) escapes from the author's language, beyond our readerly gaze. In either case he is released from the sentence of Glasgow.

If *A Chancer* works by the mutual negation of the kinds of knowledge that we expect from both first- and third-person perspectives, *The Busconductor Hines* inverts that process to elaborate alternative first- and third-person perspectives:

> What is up in his head. As heads go. He told her a lie, another fucking lie, a non-telling of the truth; and not even to explain, even attempting it, to give something almost, close to it, something as close to what was really the case, something that was the truth.[25]

Despite its apparently third-person perspective ('He told her a lie'), a paragraph such as this dissolves into the rhythm of Hines's inner consciousness, mimicking the movement of his thoughts. The immediately succeeding paragraph, however, reverses that procedure by producing a mockingly distant, third-person omniscience: 'It should be remembered, however, that Robert Hines has accomplished nought. Even the present circumstances could have been rendered more amenable.'[26] This, though, might simply be Hines commenting on himself from a third-party point of view so that the narrative consists of a dialogue between first and third persons, representing alternative possible versions of the protagonist's identity, and allowing Kelman to develop his character as a series of alternative linguistic structures. Hines is, in effect, 'sentenced' to living between conflicting sets of language games. Thus, visiting his parents, Hines is subjected to his mother's harangue that he should find his family a house in a better neighbourhood:

> Hines nodded politely as she manoeuvred her tangent.
> Why in the name of christ had he come up. He could have continued down the hill. He could have waited on and maybe gone to the broo with Griff. No. He was to be here and staying to listen to rumours concerning the housing situation in Glasgow of more than quarter of a century ago.
> Come on mammy get to the present. No. She is to ramble. People need to reiterate their facts. It makes them feel agents of a verified set, whose clear-eyed vision of the world is justly recognised by one and all. On you go hen, your wee first-born's listening quite the thing, an ever-increasing belief in your continued integrity. No.
> Stop the shite.[27]

The first sentence invokes the language of mathematics – 'manœuvred her tangent' – by which Hines regularly seeks to reduce the world to order. His mother's conversation is the product of a series of fixed expectations, like mathematical formulae – 'a verified set' – which acknowledges no alternatives, since it 'is justly recognised by one and all'. To challenge this Hines adopts a language his mother would not recognise, which starts in blasphemy – 'name of christ' – moves through economic failure – 'maybe gone to the broo' – and then to vulgarity – 'Stop the shite'. In between, Hines invokes the childhood vocabulary of a Scots vernacular which is unchallenging to his mother's social expectations: 'come on mammy,' 'on you go hen, your wee first-born's listening.' At the same time, the syntax of Hines's sentences reveal the extent to which he feels entirely determined by the world in which he is trapped; he could have done several things but 'he was to be here and staying'. The locution insists on a predeterminism in which the present and future are already as unchangeable as the past; he is not simply here – he *was* to be here. Similarly, in the present, his mother has no choice; it is part of her very being that 'she *is* to ramble.' Kelman presses language into strange syntactic structures to emphasise the extent to which, for each of us, the limits of language are the limits of our world.

Kelman's third novel, A *Disaffection* (1989), intensifies these concerns by having as its protagonist a Glasgow teacher whose teaching consists mainly in trying to subvert the rules of the educational game because he sees himself as an instrument of repression: 'He is the tool of a dictatorship government. A fellow who receives a greater than average wage for the business of fencing in the children of the suppressed poor.'[28] Patrick Doyle's inability to resolve this contradiction provokes a psychological condition in which every statement has its counterstatement, and every language game a competing set of rules which offers a different version of the real. Patrick is not so much a subject as one *subjected* to the infinite interplay of different dialects:

> So:
> so grasp the lugs and get the head battened down. And maybe she will sleep with you. Maybe she will return here, home, maybe. Maybe she will quite the thing go to bed with ye, exorcising the demons, ridding the place of its cold, its lack of human something or other – worth, value, bodily and mental togetherandatoneness for fuck sake god give the boy a break he is in fucking dreadful danger, his only recourse to a pair of electrician's pipes which he is truly thankful for amen; he is, and it is truly a blessing because most folk dont even have that, he is well aware of this and truly thankful amen lord please look down on your son and spare him, spare him, allow him to be a fellow amongst fellows and a father amongst fathers, a lover amongst lovers poor auld fucking Hölderlin I mean look at him, your man there, poor old for fuck sake and then he goes off his head, succumbs to that insanity the bastards maintain that he was only just always managing to survive from, and what about Hegel, did he help? of course he must have helped, Hegel was fucking good, good, a good ordinary man amongst men who enjoyed a bevy and a screw and a good laugh and carousing singsong with all his cronies, and at 1770 look at the fucking cronies! Beethoven for christ sake![29]

The compounded word 'togetherandatoneness' defines what is, for Doyle, an impossible condition; his thought processes constantly play between alternatives whose multiple possibilities can never be brought to a conclusion, a 'oneness'. Here a parodic version of religion ('please look down on your son') is displaced by the history of a European culture which produces madness. In the dissolution of grammatical structure it is impossible to tell whether 'your man there, poor old for fuck sake' is Hölderlin or Doyle. In language, everything is possible, and even the non-existent subsists:

> That poor old nonentity Vulcan, being once thought to exist, and then being discovered not to. Imagine being discovered not to exist! That's even worse than being declared fucking redundant, irrelevant, which was the fate of ether upon the advent of Einstein.[30]

For Patrick, there is no end to language – 'you canni stop me talking. I just talk all the time' – and no sentence can ever reach a conclusion that allows him to turn hypothesis into action, for each hypothesis, like an endless Hegelian dialectic, simply calls forth its own antithesis.[31] Doyle is sentenced *by* language to a life sentence *in* language, a tragic sufferer from the 'linguistic turn' in modern thought that sees humanity necessarily trapped in 'the prison-house of language'.[32]

Surrounded by possible meanings, Patrick both waits and fears the moment when this spiralling multiplicity of meaning will be arrested, a fear that makes him insistently conscious of the police: 'Funny how come so many officers-of-the-law crop up these days. Patrick appears to be surrounded by them. Everywhere he looks.'[33] Patrick's fear is of a language come to rest, defined in terms of a fixed relationship between words and objects – a language, that is, reduced to what philosophers describe as 'ostensive definition', in which all meanings derive from the ability to see and to point to the object which a word denotes. This is a view of language which Chomsky argues is fundamental to the British empiricist tradition, providing what thinkers such as Bertrand Russell believe to be the 'primitive or somehow basic stage in the acquisition of knowledge'. It is a theory, however, which Chomsky believes to have little credibility 'in the light of the little that is known'.[34] Patrick's fear of the finality of the ostensive provides the fundamental basis for the linguistic experiment of Kelman's fourth novel, *How late it was, how late* (1994), since its protagonist, Sammy, is someone who inhabits a vanishing world to which sight will become – quite literally – redundant. At the novel's opening Sammy comes to consciousness in a condition in which '[ye] stay there hoping yer body will disappear' but as he comes round, 'the words filling yer head, then the other words', he becomes aware that 'he was wearing an auld pair of trainer shoes for fuck sake where had they come from he had never seen them afore man auld fucking trainer shoes. The laces werenay even tied! Where was his leathers?'[35] The absent 'leathers' are prologue to a novel of vanishings. Sammy's last weekend has vanished in an alcoholic blackout; Sammy's girlfriend, Helen, has vanished; Sammy's eyesight will vanish after a beating by the police. What is vanishing, however, is that ostensive world that Chomsky believed to be the false foundation of theories of language; without sight, Sammy inhabits a world in which sound and voice have taken over from vision as the principal mode of relating to the world. As a consequence, Sammy's language is characterised not, as in the classic philosophies of Western culture, by the mimesis of the seen,[36] but by an elaborate process of *anticipation*, in which language, like Sammy's white stick, goes on ahead of him, filling in the time to come with expectation:

Silence. Then the music blared again so the inside door had been opened; maybe there was more of them, more of the bastards; he shook the stick, getting his wrists relaxed. Quiet voices quiet voices, he was gony have to move man he was gony have to fucking move, now, he stepped back, pushing out the door and out onto the pavement he went left, tapping as quick as he could, keeping into the wall. He hit against somebody but battered on, just to keep going, he was fine man he was okay except this feeling like any minute the wallop from behind, the blow in the back, the quick rush of air then thud, he kept going, head down, the shoulders hunched. There was a lane, he turned down it and went a way along then stopped. He was breathing hard. A fucking mug man that was what he was, that was all he was, a mug, a fucking mug. He walked on a few paces then stopped again. A fucking mug.[37]

Released from the ostensive fixities of sight, Sammy's language anticipates possibilities – 'this feeling like any minute the wallop from behind' – which, since they are not fulfilled, lead his language into a process of repetition and elaboration, a circling of words in search of definition and in search of an object on which to fix themselves: 'A fucking mug man that was what he was, that was all he was, a mug, a fucking mug.'

By making Sammy blind Kelman makes Glasgow effectively disappear into its language, as fluid and indefinable as the terms which attempt to locate Sammy himself, shifting as they do from 'ye', to 'I', to 'he' and back to 'Sammy'. As a consequence, Sammy's language does not chart the real but invokes people, objects and events into existence:

The doors [of the lift] closed. Up he went. This is fucking lovely! he said. And he made a coughing sound like he was clearing his throat. It was a cover-up for the fact he had spoke out loud. He knew there was naybody in the lift with him but it was probably fucking bugged man know what I'm talking about, or else a VCR, probably there was a VCR. And that security cunt was sitting watching him right at this very minute, having a wee laugh to himself cause Sammy was talking and there was naybody there. Aye fuck you, he said and moved his head around, Fuck you.[38]

The speculative security man looking at the VCR image becomes an address-able 'you', as real as any other inhabitant of a world which Sammy has con-stantly to imagine into existence. In this context, language revolves in the repetition of oral formulations which have no actual reference in the world; 'Aye fuck you [. . .] Fuck you' is a defence against the visual that would fix Sammy – 'watching him right at this very minute' – in the certainty of a once-and-for-all event in a determined world. The popular criticisms which counted the number of times 'fuck' was repeated in the novel, as though this was a sign of Kelman's lack of linguistic creativity, missed the point, for repetition is the only possible organising principle of language when it is divorced from the fixity of the visual. Sammy's language works by an incanta-tory repetition of phrases which develop a reality of their own:

But it couldnay get worse than this. He was really fuckt now. This was the dregs; he was at it. He had fucking reached it now man the fucking dregs man the pits, the fucking black fucking limboland, purgatory; that's what it was like, purgatory, where all ye can do is think. Think. That's all ye can do. Ye just think about what ye've done and what ye've no fucking done; ye cannay look at nothing ye cannay see nothing it's just a total fucking disaster area, yer mind, yer fucking memories, a disaster area.[39]

'Fuckt' invokes 'the fucking black limboland' which invokes 'purgatory' which is defined as 'where all ye can do is think'. Language is here shaped not by its contact with an external reality but by its exfoliation into more language. Sammy is a walking vernacular dictionary, defining words by other words, and revealing that language, and therefore human life, rests upon an existential nothingness; if it is the case that 'ye cannay look at nothing ye cannay see nothing,' 'nothingness' may nevertheless be there. Standard language, by having rules which give us the illusion of a shared and stable world, conceals the nothingness from which language emerges; dialect, by breaking those rules, unveils the emptiness from which standard language defends us. Sammy's language turns a social misfit (who has almost nothing) into an existential quester (confronting nothingness).

In each of Kelman's early novels we are given characters whose 'dialect' is both the expression of their freedom, their ability to break rules, and, at the same time, the establishment of the limits of their world. Each of them, however, also exists in Kelman's literary language, a language which, in the end, is their determining medium. Sammy's refusal of external control is also a refusal to submit to that linguistic identity: 'Sammy wanted to vanish. Jesus christ he wanted to vanish, he really did' – and really does.[40] *How late it was, how late* enacts the absorption of reality into language and, in its conclusion, the escape from language into . . . what? Action? Freedom? Silence? We cannot know because we, as readers, have only the world of language, sentenced to retrace the meanings and the environment from which Sammy has escaped. We, rather than he, remain the prisoners of a Glasgow sentence.

CHAPTER EIGHT

Kelman's Art-Speech

Scott Hames

During the 1994 controversy over Kelman's Booker Prize, the Tory politician and columnist Alan Clark described the winning novel as

> a 'book' – Compiled? Scripted? I am trying to avoid the word 'written' – by a Glaswegian [which] consists of a series of transcripts taken from a running tape (there can be no other explanation) of a maundering old drunk.[1]

This description is inaccurate in almost every respect, but it shows with particular clarity the impulse to deny the *writtenness* of Kelman's fiction. This sounds absurd, but like many other critics at the time, Clark wanted to deny 'literary' status to the language and protagonist of *How late it was, how late* (see Chapter 2). The image of Kelman patching the novel together from scraps of 'real' conversation is meant to devalue and limit his role to that of a faithful reporter, a kind of cultural stenographer who records, copies and transcribes from direct experience (as opposed to a literary artist who crafts, sculpts and invents, using his imagination). Clark's effort to disprove Kelman's literariness draws on deeply ingrained cultural imagery about language, whereby speech is regarded as authentic but guileless, and writing as skilled artifice. Because skilled artifice is, according to Clark's prejudices, wholly incongruous with the social milieu of *How late*, 'there can be no other explanation' but that Kelman merely duplicates actual talk. When he runs out of grim tales and colourful idioms, Kelman can simply return to the pub with a bucket and hoist some fresh patter up from the well.

This is an egregious case, but Clark is far from the only critic to treat Kelman as some kind of passive transmitter of the Real. Kelman recalls the earliest critical response to his work, as part of Philip Hobsbaum's extra-mural writing group in the early 1970s:

> Occasionally textual suggestions were made as though they never would have occurred to me. There was a vague assumption that the stories had just come. All I did was write them down. It was weird. I sweated blood over the damn

things. Seventeen years later my novel A *Disaffection* was shortlisted for prizes and a member of an adjudicating panel asked if I ever revised 'or did it just come out?'

It jist comes oot, ah says, it's the natchril rithm o the workin klass, ah jist opens ma mooth and oot it comes. Similar to the American dancer in reply to a related question, ah jes closes ma eyes an ma feets git to movin.[2]

Dozens of books and awards later, this misreading is with us still. As the novelist James Meek recently observed, 'a generous but misdirected romanticism [. . .] would like to imagine Kelman warbling his native fucknotes wild, simply sluicing a measure of his authentic working-class soul onto the page.'[3] There is far more art to Kelman's work, and to his language, than the persistence of this image would suggest. To put it simply, Kelman's work cannot be reduced to *mimesis* (imitation); it is quite as much the product of *poiesis* (making, shaping), and it engenders a certain aesthetic *distance* from 'real' or 'natural' language. This chapter will not waste time disproving what is self-evidently bigoted and fanciful in the image of Kelman-as-stenographer. Instead, it will explore Kelman's own preferred image as a language artist: a writer highly conscious of his methods and techniques, who makes rather than reproduces the verbal forms we encounter in his fiction. Too often, this dimension of his work is obscured by the journalistic cliché linking Kelman to 'gritty' social realism.

I

This shift in perspective – from *mimesis* to *poiesis* – runs against the grain of the 'elementary matter of [Kelman's] chosen artform, language'.[4] We need to spend a moment understanding this pattern before turning to Kelman's work. The most important of Kelman's linguistic materials is the Glasgow vernacular – vernacular meaning in this context 'the native speech of a populace, in contrast to another or others acquired for commercial, social, or educative purposes'[5] – and vernacular writing is freighted with powerful associations of authenticity and verisimilitude. It seems to plug directly into the 'real' language of 'real' people. This aura of 'truthiness' is not natural or inherent to the vernacular, but *ascribed* to it over a long period of history, partly as a compensation for being de-legitimised during the emergence of Standard English, and partly as a residue of the Romantic vogue for 'the real language of men'. Both these factors are encoded in the narrative conventions of the realist novel, where English that deviates from the written standard is conventionally employed to individualise, typify and ironise character voices. Local dialect, slang and 'unliterary' language function as a source of comedy, concreteness and local colour, and as an index of social and regional difference. By contrast, the standard, non-localised language of the narrator is affiliated to a controlling narrative discourse which operates above the 'given' and evident reality of the fictive world. It 'shows' the 'object-discourse' of the fictive world – the activities, perspectives and languages of characters – without ever itself being shown, and 'functions simply as a window on reality'.[6] Since the 'meta-narrative' of the realist novel in English (the 'unwritten' prose-window on fictive reality) is almost always presented in Standard English (the non-localised model for English speech and writing), their functions and associations are routinely, unconsciously, conflated. And thanks to the powerful determining influence of the novel on our ways of perceiving writing in general, all Standard English prose tends to bear this aura of weightless transparency and meta-discursivity. In Kelman's critical writing, this conflation and its lasting impact go by the name of 'Standard English Literary Form'.[7] Despite the sinister capital letters, we should realise that Kelman is not simply declaring war on the associations and values crystallised by 'SELF' – at least not head-on. The unsettling and estranging effects of his work depend upon, and manipulate, readers' internalisation of these connotations; they are the canvas of his verbal art.

To outline briefly the readerly implications of internalising 'SELF': we tend unconsciously to process textually 'deviant' language as 'object discourse' directly opening onto a given, self-evident reality. We read a non-standard word – 'wos' for 'was' – as a transcription of actual talking: as outward, empirical speech, rather than a narrator's interior reflection. This effect works in concert with 'phonocentrism', the Western tendency to equate speech with presence and substance deconstructed by Jacques Derrida.[8] We associate the vernacular sign with the 'naturalness' and naïvety of characters ignorant of the linguistic norms they fail to conform to, and subject to highly localised, particularised perspectives (with their attendant strengths and weaknesses, e.g. rootedness and narrowness). Perhaps most importantly, we are hasty to read non-standard language as possessing material density and opacity, and to interpret it as the concrete embodiment – not the sign – of socio-cultural difference. The speaker of 'wos' is instantly specific and located.

These 'authenticity effects' contain a crucial irony, highlighted in the phoneticised rendering of 'natchril rithms' in the passage cited earlier. Representing the vernacular on its own terms – unmediated by the standard language and orthography, which constantly threaten to colonise and suppress it – entails a novel and self-validating approach to representing speech (that is, an approach which does not seem overly indebted to the standard conventions). But the earthy, 'natural' language produced by all such techniques constantly and paradoxically flags its *strangeness and artificiality as writing*. Far from appearing self-originating and essential – natural – the vernacular text appears opaque, ersatz: the synthetic product of an arbitrary code. This is not to sell the Romantic strengths of the vernacular short – its capacity, in Tom Paulin's words, to generate 'authenticity that bonds the reader in an intimate, personal matter'.[9] 'Contrary to the assumption governing the realist tradition,' Derek Attridge writes of Joyce, 'an even stronger sense of the physically and emotionally real can be created in language that foregrounds its own materiality.'[10] But language that foregrounds its own materiality is inevitably, at the level of realist narrative discourse, foregrounding its own signifying activity, and hence its apartness from the solid objects (and 'object discourses') of the fictive world.

This paradox of vernacular authenticity, and the effects to which Kelman puts it, bring us within the orbit of a crucial twentieth-century debate concerning the *aesthetic* dimension of language. The remainder of this chapter will outline an alternative perspective to the speech-naturalism paradigm typified by Clark, which tends to deny Kelman the distance from actuality – from the given, from what *is* – his work demands both formally and ethically. By deliberately over-emphasising this dimension of Kelman's work, I mean to challenge the simplistic image of his unswerving commitment to verisimilitude.

II

It is telling that Kelman should describe his seminal story 'Nice to be nice' as '[his] earliest attempt at the *literary or phonetic* transcription of a speaking voice' (my emphasis).[11] Getting the story right took dozens of drafts (see Chapter 1), but linguistic accuracy was not the ultimate goal, or treated as an end in itself; the enterprise was literary before it was phonetic. Kelman has expressed irritation with critical responses which make the 'means of expression' the 'primary concern', while 'the thing expressed is irrelevant.'[12] Language is an artistic medium with which he means to *create* something; establishing the 'validity' of the medium is necessary, but insufficient. This is an essential point in grasping the aesthetic dimension of Kelman's interest in orality, dialect and the speaking voice. Kelman is a realist *artist*; he does not ventriloquise an unselfconscious 'oral culture' engaged in 'natural' verbal activity. Moreover, Kelman's linguistic innovations are not essentially about 'directness' – are not attempts to bypass the conventions of 'Standard English Literary Form' to inscribe 'social content' directly into text, achieving a kind of unmediated authenticity. The seemingly 'raw' and artless features of Kelman's vernacular are in fact the most stylised and deliberately crafted.

Take this passage from *You Have to be Careful in the Land of the Free*, in which the protagonist Jeremiah Brown is describing a conversation with two tramps who hang around the airport where he works as a security guard:

> I was quite into it but the mair excited Homer and Jethro became the mair their
> brains launched into these outer-cosmic tales of supranatooral magic, mystery
> and hobgoblins. Nay wonder with that 147-proof rotgut they drank. Baith liked
> wonderful books about inner-earth goodies and netherworld baddies and wee
> boys that outwitted baleful sorcerers. They were of the opinion that the world
> 'as we know it' could never go forward until having returned to the true values
> of Lancelot, Guinevere and the Knights of the Round Table.[13]

Long-standing conventions of realist fiction tend to allocate such idiosyncratic
language to the speech of colourful minor characters – characters like Homer
and Jethro. But here it is the narrative idiom – the 'diegetic' voice which *tells*
the story, rather than being *shown* by some narrative meta-language – which
is saturated with 'locality', quirkiness and strangeness. Recognisable Scottish
forms evoking a 'rooted' narrative persona (e.g. 'mair', 'nay', 'baith') seem to
authenticate this voice in accordance with the pattern noted above; but other
features of this narrative idiom seem to *dis*-authenticate the storytelling voice,
to present it as stilted and artificial (e.g. the perfective verb-phrase 'until having
returned to'). Mock-ceremonious use of 'high', literary and formal registers of
English is a common feature of Kelman's writing, but the target or direction of
the irony we detect here ('baleful sorcerers') is uncertain; the clichés of fantasy
fiction are gently signalled by 'wonderful books', i.e. books full of the wondrous
and 'supranatooral', but also 'wonderful!' as a complacent middlebrow evaluation of such writing. Like the 'going forward' achieved by the return to medi-
eval romance, the various textures of this passage pull us in different directions;
the result is stranger and more unsettling, in narrative terms, than anything to
be found in Harry Potter. The world 'as we know it' feels very remote; we are
immersed in a deeply (if unevenly) stylised fictive universe, estranged from the
protocols of 'straight' realism usually crystallised by the presence of vernacular
writing as 'object discourse' (superintended by 'SELF'). There is no reference
point by which we might gain our bearings to 'truth' or 'true values', no solid
reality in excess of 'voice' against which to measure its fidelity.

To be sure, Kelman is better known for employing an artful stylisation of
aural features to heighten, rather than scramble, realistic description:

> Ye might want to smile but it's fuck all to smile about, it's just reality, so ye face
> up to it, know what I mean if ye've nay choice man, it's a head-down situation.
> Christ he was shaking, shaking. Stop it. He couldnay stop it. Aye he could. He
> got up off the bed and took four babysteps forwards, four babysteps backwards,
> just getting the breathing, just getting that, okay, then the jeans, pulling them
> on, balancing with one hand against the wall; then the tee-shirt.[14]

Kelman here uses aural effects to *dramatise* Sammy's experience: the rhythms
of this passage from *How late it was, how late* embody the character's anxiety

and his physical and emotional efforts to control it. Staccato variation of phrase-lengths and use of repetition force the reader to adjust the flow of his or her own mental 'breathing', and bring us into fretful harmony with Sammy's condition. We are made to feel what is described. Self-evidently, the author is using language as a flexible material he can mould in order to achieve specific effects. Far from being a passive conduit of language whose untainted 'authenticity' is paramount, Kelman is up to his elbows shaping and crafting the linguistic impressions his work makes on us, often ambushing our routine ways of processing verbal form. This reminds us that language is *used* rather than lived, and is never simply the 'embodiment' of cultural identity or experience. 'There is something very bewitching about the assumption that our cultural identity is somehow locked up inside our language,' writes Bill Ashcroft, 'that there is some natural and organic relation between language and culture.'[15] On the contrary, 'language is not simply a repository of cultural contents, but a tool, and often a weapon, which can be employed for various purposes, *a tool which is itself part of the cultural experience in which it is used*' (my emphasis).[16] As we shall see, the difficulty of abstracting language from the social reality in which it is used is a challenge for any attempt to mount an aesthetic perspective on vernacular forms. For now, it is enough to notice that language is both the medium and the subject of Kelman's art, which not only manipulates the English language, but also the reader's internalised linguistic habits, in order to achieve heightened and stylised effects.

The range of these verbal effects has often been overlooked. For example, most of the inner monologue cited above is mimetically 'convincing'; we can readily imagine Sammy Samuels thinking these thoughts. But elsewhere in the novel aural features play a very different role:

> He got down on his knees to feel the floor, cold but firm, cold but firm. The palms of his hands flat on it; he had this sensation of being somewhere else in the world and a music started in his head, a real real music, it was hypnotic, these instruments beating out the tumatumatumti tumatumatumti tum, tum; tum, ti tum; tum, tum; tum, ti tum, tumatumatumti tumatumatumti byong; byong byong byong byong byong; byong, byong byong, byong, byong byong. He was down now and rolled onto his back, lying there smiling, then with his face screwed up; shooting pains.[17]

This 'real real music' works by refiguring the narrative language as raw aurality. Instead of a window on the fictive universe, the language of Sammy's story *becomes* the story, an 'instrument' performing rather than describing his perceptions. The verbal paint lays thick and opaque; Kelman has 'estranged' the frame through which we orient ourselves to the text and its protocols of representation. We become acutely conscious of language as a factor in its own right, mediating our experience of the character's reality, and we also become attuned to the aural, non-verbal dimension of language itself: its physical noisiness. Sammy is not thinking but listening, and in this scene we listen alongside him. This is 'real real music' in so far as it suspends the realist meta-discourse, in which the narrative language has no materiality, is the product of no articulation.

Is this a deepening and heightening of realism, or a departure from it? There is a *verismo* effect here – an evocation of the 'actual' noise inside Sammy's head, presumably linked to the 'shooting pains' – but one that draws on the imaginative sympathy of the reader's 'inner ear', not any possible 'objective' recording scenario. We are close, then, to the 'Romantic dream of words that perfectly speak of the inner human world'.[18] Kelman's characteristic focus on the moment-to-moment drama of the inner life draws on a Romantic inheritance (most explicitly in A *Disaffection*), including Wordsworth's aim to compose poetry in 'the real language of men'.[19] Derek Attridge paraphrases Wordsworth's prediction in the 'Preface' to *Lyrical Ballads*, the most famous statement on art-speech in English,

> that readers of the poems that follow will have to 'struggle with feelings of strangeness and awkwardness'. The argument is clear, if obliquely stated: what passes for poetry in Wordsworth's time is not a reflection of the 'real' language of men but an artificial confection which has become so dominant that the response to his very different poetry – from which that 'real' language will shine out undimmed – will be bemusement and dismay.[20]

Hence one account of the strangeness of the Real; the familiar conventions are so divorced from reality, and yet so determining of our perceptions, reality seems peculiar. This is one available argument about vernacular writing which Kelman, at times, seems to endorse, stating that 'writing the way people talk' only seems peculiar because of the rigid enforcement of an unspoken prohibition against it.[21] We can also, however, see Kelman from the contrasting perspective, one which allocates a different role to linguistic oddness, enabling a more liberating vision of the vernacular aesthetic. Rather than viewing Kelman's project in accordance with the Romantic paradigm, as faithfully 'including' the real language of men within high literary form (or generating new literary forms to accommodate the real language of men), we can regard him embracing artifice and exploring stylisation: of dealing in the 'peculiar language' of art, at some remove from reality.

III

The Russian Formalist critic Viktor Shklovsky theorised that 'the artistic quality of something, its relationship to poetry [as opposed to mundane prose], is a result of our mode of perception,' not that something's own intrinsic qualities.[22] The role of art, therefore, is to refresh perception, which is forever in danger of going stale, becoming habitual and automatic. Art for Shklovsky is 'a way of restoring conscious experience, of breaking through deadening and mechanical habits of conduct' in general.[23] By 'defamiliaris-ing' humdrum reality and our routinised ways of processing it, art shakes us out of our lethargy to remind us that perception is an *active* process. The works best suited to this purpose are wilfully artificial, forcing us into con-scious, protracted awareness of their styles, materials and forms, thwarting lazy 'naturalisation' of recognised conventions:

> By 'enstranging' objects and complicating form, the device of art makes percep-tion long and 'laborious'. The perceptual process has a purpose all its own and ought to be extended to the fullest. *Art is a means of experiencing the process of creativity.*[24]

The friction, the effort, the *opacity* of vernacular writing is aesthetically freeing on just these terms; reading and becoming conscious of the labour of reading is a different, more acute mode of literary perception than merely parsing recognised words treated (automatically, i.e. unconsciously) as ciphers of verbal 'content'. 'The hallmark of the artistic', by this logic, is an 'artifact that has been intentionally removed from the domain of automa-tized perception', awakening us to its eligibility for transformation.[25] But can 'natural' speech really be the basis of such artifacts? Fredric Jameson's para-phrase of the Formalist position invites us to consider Kelman's vernacular effects in the light of Shklovskian *ostranit'* – 'enstrangement':

> The Formalists began by demonstrating that in many ways poetic speech stood to everyday language as a type of dialect [. . .] A poetic language which is a dialect is one which attracts attention to itself, and such attention results in renewed perception of the very material quality of language itself.[26]

Let us turn this figure inside out. If literary language is a 'dialect' of ordi-nary language, does dialect writing – even 'unpoetic' dialect writing – not partake of precisely the same effects, renewing verbal perception simply by virtue of being 'opaque' vis-à-vis the standard language and orthography? Does 'doesnay' not attract attention to itself in the way Shklovsky suggests is 'poetic', just as 'natchril', 'mair' and 'baith' did in earlier examples?

Like Shklovsky's 'poetic speech', vernacular writing 'is "artificially" created by an artist in such a way that the perceiver, pausing in his reading, dwells on the text. This is when the literary work attains its greatest and most long-lasting impact.'[27] The perceptual weirdness of dialect, vernacular or non-standard forms – of what Dora Ahmad simply calls (after Ken Saro-Wiwa) 'Rotten English' – begins to take on the complexion of the definitive verbal aesthetic. Rather than being 'more real' than art, and bypassing signification to incarnate naturalness and authenticity, the vernacular text becomes the touchstone of an *autonomous* literary medium founded in perceptual friction and self-consciousness:

> According to Aristotle, poetic language ought to have the character of something foreign, something outlandish about it. [. . .] All things considered, we've arrived at a definition of poetry as the language of *impeded, distorted* speech.[28]

'Homely' language is textually 'foreign' in just this way, permitting Kelman to access a curious double register of estrangement. It pulls now toward Shklovskian de-automatisation – a self-conscious refreshing of verbal perception – and now toward the authenticity of a 'natural' language unspoilt by social convention or linguistic propriety: a Romantic language *exempt* from automatisation because it supposedly springs directly from nature.

This tension has a history. The 'plainer and more emphatic language' Wordsworth adopts from 'low and rustic life' for the *Lyrical Ballads* is held to transcend verbal artifice (and 'fickle tastes' for its passing fashions) by its close contact with elemental nature. This 'real language of men' embodies 'the passions of men [. . .] incorporated with the beautiful and permanent forms of nature', from which that language ultimately derives.[29] 'What had to be kept at bay in this account', Attridge writes, 'was the old idea of poet as craftsman, since every conscious decision about a word places a distance between the poet's language and the real language of men produced spontaneously in states of passion.'[30] The vernacular is thus poised between maximal and minimal aesthetic distance from the Real; it signifies both nature itself and self-conscious artifice.

On one hand, vernacular strangeness – deviation from 'SELF' – entails laborious reading, self-conscious textuality and (when used as the narrative language) a smudge on the window of realist meta-discourse. On the other, Kelman eschews Romantic voice by *throwing the vernacular back on itself*. Its strangeness is almost never allowed to consolidate a new, competing standard, to attain settled discursive authority (as object- or meta-language), or the consolations of 'homeliness' as a rooted language of origins. So Kelman is not any kind of 'straight' realist, and his approach to language is not, despite the journalistic consensus, naturalistic. There is no 'real' speech in Kelman; 'real real music' takes its place – language estranged from routine orthographic cipherment and encountered as a series of fresh perceptual events. This flow of language is 'real' twice over: once for evading assimilation to dominant conventions, preserving authenticity (as in the MTV sense of 'keeping it real'), twice for *making us conscious* of the Romantic protocols of 'keeping it real' (i.e. the textual sleight-of-hand for *making* it real), and partly disowning them.

To put this another way, Kelman's vernacular is both SELF-estranged (deviating from Standard English Literary Form) and *self*-estranged, in so far as it scrambles the organicism of Romantic vocal 'presence'. The second of these effects is more difficult to observe, because it is realised from *within* the forms of a recognised folk-art of the quotidian (dialect fiction). But this should not blind us to the fact that the vital tension in Kelman's work lies between the aura of vocal territoriality – the sense of a 'located' social speech being faithfully reproduced – and a distancing stylisation of 'real language': an aestheticisation of the demotic which secures a degree of *freedom* from the empirical and given, opening the way to a readerly experience of creativity and possibility.

It is not only at the level of linguistic method that Kelman explores the artificial dimension of 'natural' and organic cultural forms. We can see him link this linguistic problem to a wider aesthetic agenda in A *Disaffection*, questioning, in a pair of vital images, the possibility of artistic exceptionalism – the 'peculiar' object which renews and liberates perception, against the backdrop of mundane routine – and the possibility of an autonomous folk-art rooted in the 'given' and recognised forms of a community.

IV

When Patrick discovers the 'pair of old pipes' in the opening scene of A *Disaffection*, great emphasis is placed upon his initial perceptions and associations. First evoking 'english saxophones from a bygone era', they trigger a lengthy digression about the protagonist's 'secret hankering' to be a painter; description of the physical objects swerves into inward speculation on the possibility of being an artist.[31] This pattern is repeated in the narrative syntax: 'the pipes were strange kind of objects in the response Patrick had for them.'[32] The second half of this sentence transforms the first; we never encounter the pipes in their own right, but always mediated by Patrick's imaginative perception of them. The 'strangeness' is his, not theirs, and we are left guessing what these pipes are *really* – that is, what they are really *for*. The would-be artist places them in an aesthetic context long before they are affixed to a 'given' functional identity (as 'ordinary pipes like the sort used by plumbers and electricians'[33]). Even before he decides to possess them, before their physical characteristics have been specified, Patrick makes a sort of test performance 'round the back' of the local arts centre. The pipes are thus poised between 'ordinary' and 'aesthetic' purposes and contexts from the moment we encounter them; they hover on this threshold for the entirety of the novel. When his re-appearance with the pipes raises the eyebrows of his work colleagues, Patrick can only reply 'they'll come in handy,' without specifying how.[34]

The pipes are emblems of aesthetic possibility which constantly register the pressure of the ordinary and the practical. Reflecting on his own half-conscious project of 'transforming commercially produced products into aesthetic weapons', Patrick concedes 'any person could recognise the pipes for what they were and good luck to them.'[35] Presenting them as musical instruments rather than industrial tools creates a 'distance' from recognised reality which Patrick initially distrusts (as escapist 'conceptualising'), but which he gradually experiences, in the moment of performance, as a profound release from his fraught inner life.[36] His intense self-consciousness is only relieved when consciously *heightened* via aesthetic ritual:

> Enter yourself ya bastard. Play the fucker. Before it is too late. Fine. What is done is just that Patrick raises the pipe to his lips and closes his eyelids; he blows a very long and very deep sound; just one, lips compressed, eyelids shut tightly, and tears springing there at the corners, like a form of ecstasy, something that has sprung from way out of and has relaxed these shoulders and eased that terrible terrible fucking tension, just got out from under that pilloriedness, self-pilloriedness, self-flagellation [. . .] just there, there, there, getting further and further away, not a great distance but a distance, definitely a distance[. . .][37]

This capacity to engender aesthetic distance – to suspend temporarily the tyranny of what-is – explains the pipes' correlation with freedom, possibility and escape ('With these pipes in tow anything was possible. Nay! Probable!'[38]). If the pipes themselves hover between the fixed and the contingent – Patrick at first agonises about tampering with their 'selfcolour', of supplementing or distracting from their 'actual physicality'[39] – the aesthetic experience they make possible turns the 'given' against its own paralysing sameness by artificially exaggerating it: sustaining one note for long enough to become immersed in concrete sound to the exclusion of all else. This artificial distance ('it was more like a sort of breathing space, that he was producing'[40]), this self-conscious suspension of the actual *via absorption in its sensuous particularity* is, in Kelman, the precondition of possibility and freedom. Questioning the 'thingness' of the pipes themselves forms part of this awareness ('But what about the pipes? Were they things? Were the pipes things?'[41]), in language which cannot but evoke the provocation of René Magritte's painting 'The Treachery of Images' (1928–9), in which a stock figure of an 'ordinary' pipe is countered by the text *Ceci n'est pas une pipe* (*This is not a pipe*). Word, image and 'thing' fail to correspond; the statement is literally true, since the referent is a painting rather than a pipe, but having the unspoken protocols of representational art challenged so baldly goes beyond literalism, to insist the space of the painting is irreducibly *figural*. And so with writing. We must never forget that texts are composed of signs, and that the various reality-effects of Kelman's writing (including voice) are the product of artifice: 'critics and arbiters of art must understand the need for caution [. . .] all technique is metaphor.'[42]

A different kind of problem is engendered by the *social* basis of an art form with language for its material. Elsewhere in *A Disaffection*, Kelman broaches the question of art-speech by alluding to another modernist text of the 1920s:

> I am the Piper Doyle. I pipe. Up piped Doyle to enliven the proceedings. That story of Kafka's about the nice wee woman who is a vain mouse and who pipes a song of astonishing, of astonishing
> Astonishing what for fuck sake I've fucking forgotten.[43]

Kafka's last finished story, 'Josephine the Singer' (1924), concerns the status of a folk-art indistinguishable from ordinary verbal communication: a 'piping' which is symbolic of collective origins and identity, but solemnly 'performed' by an individual aspiring to aesthetic singularity. Through a series of elaborate reflections on this art, Kafka's 'narrator dismantles all Josephine's claims to being exceptional but is able to discern the special qualities of her performance in its exaggerated ordinariness':[44]

> Among intimates we admit freely to one another that Josephine's singing, as singing, is nothing out of the ordinary.
> Is it in fact singing at all? [. . .] Is it not perhaps just a piping? And piping is something we all know about, it is the real artistic accomplishment of our people, or rather no mere accomplishment but a characteristic expression of our life. We all pipe, but of course no one dreams of making out that our piping is an art [. . .] Yet if you sit down before her, it is not merely a piping; to comprehend her art it is necessary not only to hear but to see her. Even if hers were only our usual workaday piping, there is first of all this peculiarity to consider, that here is someone making a ceremonial performance out of doing the usual thing.[45]

The politics of cultural representation enter this complex reckoning; if Josephine is styled as the iconic performer of the mouse-folk's characteristic piping, is her lyric individuality not cancelled by this symbolic role?

> It is not so much a performance of songs as an assembly of the people [. . .] This piping, which rises up where everyone else is pledged to silence, comes almost like a message from the whole people to each individual.[46]

Note that the origin of this message is social rather than personal. There is, here, no possibility for expressivity in the Romantic sense – no space in which 'voice' could embody subjectivity or register peculiarity. The smothering self-identity of this social language seems to prohibit all estrangement. In her quest for 'permanent recognition of her art', Josephine threatens to 'cut short her grace notes'; 'presumably she has carried out her threat,' the narrator reports, 'although I for one have observed no difference in her performance.'[47] Josephine 'denies any connection between her art and ordinary piping', but the strange social power of her performance stems precisely from its aesthetic failure: 'she gets effects which a trained singer would try in vain to achieve among us and which are only produced precisely because her means are so inadequate.'[48] Wholly saturated with 'we-ness', this medium is never susceptible to individual 'enlivenment' or stylistic heightening; its totalising 'sociality' leaves no room for idiosyncrasy.

V

This is a nightmare-vision of authentically 'rooted' art-speech, and Kelman refuses it. His art is about trying to seize autonomy and freedom from given realities, not just reproducing them objectively. His art insists on fidelity to the actual – early in A *Disaffection* Patrick upbraids himself 'to concentrate solely upon things of genuine value, things of a genuine authenticity, of a genuine physicality'[49] – but never wallows in the self-presence of the Real. The challenge, which none of Kelman's protagonists fully meets, is not to become so firmly anchored in what-is as to hamstring efforts to transform it; to achieve some condition of difference or possibility *from within its reality*. The novelty of the common, the strangeness of the actual – this is the aesthetic territory on which Kelman stages the politics of language and realism. Verisimilitude – or, as it appears in Kelman's mischievous tale of erroneous transcription, 'versailintude' – comes a distant second to verbal creativity: 'how could it be a mistake if it was my very own, and why not just a new creation altogether?'[50]

CHAPTER NINE

Kelman and World English

Michael Gardiner

In *The World Republic of Letters*, Pascale Casanova groups James Kelman, Tom Leonard and Alasdair Gray together as establishing a 'new idiom' through 'the *littérarisation* of oral practices'.[1] Casanova describes a grouping which is discrete by having 'managed through the illustration and defence of a popular language – affirmed as a specifically Scottish mode of expression – to create a difference that was both social and national.'[2] The local is linked to the global via the systematic nature of cultural capital, and nations accumulate status, authority and legitimacy via recognition by literary institutions of global reach. Classic works and characteristic styles then become distinctive and are 'nationalised' to serve as models. This means that the differentiating function of a national literature depends less on the achievements of the singular genius than on the sameness of its institutional productions of a model, and national tradition is the demand to compete for distinctness, marketing literary products along ethnic lines. Frequently Scottish literature is divided into schools along these lines and prepared for a global literary marketplace, so that the political contestations surrounding devolution are presented merely as a kind of corrective.[3] Franco Moretti and critics influenced by World Systems Theory point towards an alternative 'rise of the novel' which contravenes the organic telling of literary historical evolution at the core by being based on comparable forms at the peripheries.[4] This perspective challenges the assumption that literary form arises in the core culture, and then native content simply adapts to it at the periphery:

> There is, then, a certain reading of literary works of which only writers on the periphery are capable; certain homologies and similarities that they alone, as a result of their outlying position, are able to discern [. . .] The choices made by dominated writers with regard to language – decisions that are neither conscious nor calculated – do not consist, as in the great literary nations, in docile submission to a national norm [. . .][5]

An obvious problem when relating all this to English is that the core field which attributes value – English Literature – is not properly national at all;

it only takes off when English becomes absorptive rather than discrete, and develops as a product of a nationless state whose claims to discreteness have long been in decline. This leaves the question of a politics of the periphery that escapes the statist demand to sell ethnicity in global markets, as markets are conceived by Casanova. It is telling in this sense that Kelman's 1994 Booker Prize was quickly construed in the British media in terms of multiculturalism, and a Britishness which manages a range of national productions. Julia Neuberger's 'crap' comment is now well known (see Chapter 2), but Simon Jenkins was more revealing in his own negative review which stated 'I'm glad Mr. Kelman is a cultural pluralist.'[6] Only some linguistic forms are seen as colourful manifestations of internal difference; Jenkins's comment on cultural pluralism is unlikely to be made of Martin Amis or Julian Barnes. Since the literary qualities then are seen as not innate, but subject to a translation process in terms of 'pluralism', the difference itself is what becomes marketable here on Casanova's terms, the national.

The peripheral author then also typically has to make herself visible, to become an embodied guarantor of 'vernacular' authenticity;[7] the British press frequently relies on descriptions of Kelman *himself* as gruff, angry, committed, as a noble savage possessed of a miraculous and self-taught sensibility. An example is Nicholas Wroe's *Guardian* profile of 2001, in which, although loudly disdainful of universities (and despite having accepted public funds both as an undergraduate and as faculty), Kelman is 'better and more broadly read than most of [Mia Carter's] colleagues [at the University of Texas]'.[8] In this model, Kelman's role has become a Romantic and Ossianic one of standing outside of core English to feed it with authentic vernacular. It is a familiar trope in which the literary forms of the core culture are quietly propped up by a stream of peripheral content; as well as being globally common, it is also particularly British, feeds into the idea of organic form, and is apposite to an unwritten constitution for which political events are never seen as actions but are defined retrospectively in terms of how they have been absorbed. But in practice Kelman is a terrible choice as an Ossianic figure of authenticity. The more biographical we get, drawing in evidence from other kinds of texts, the more confused this becomes. Statements of Kelman's taken by critics as explaining themes in the fiction often ramble and contradict themselves, working along dialectical lines of thought until stumbling on a point of uncertainty, then doubling back. There is little coherence, and, outside of the realms of the biographical-diagnostic habits of Eng Lit, there is no reason why there should be coherence. The voice has much more in common with perpetual revolution in Jean-Paul Sartre than with organic form in T. S. Eliot, and the desire to fix Kelman's comments to a single authorial stance itself reveals a British-ideological need to individuate and ethnicise – 'tradition and the individual talent'.

Indeed much critical writing on world literary language – and in this Casanova is joined by Ismail Talib's study of global literary English – tends to repeat two of the major tenets of those literary disciplines which are, like Eng Lit, centred on nations as ethnic entities managed by states. Firstly, it tends to diagnose work biographically in terms of an authorial vision; and secondly, it demands that writers represent their own region in a global market. Talib's otherwise useful guide to literary language descends into the weakest kind of tribal ethnic claims when it comes to 'Literature in English by the non-English in Britain':

> Today, and in the past, the indigenous non-English people of the British Isles often display hostility towards England and the English, for they believe that the politically dominant English and their language will destroy or corrupt their own language or culture.[9]

Kelman's post-Booker fiction presents serious difficulties to ethnic readings of the work as a whole. There is a clear shift of scenes between *How late it was, how late* (1994) to *Translated Accounts* (2001) and then *You Have to be Careful in the Land Of The Free* (2004), which, since the action leaves Scotland, has sometimes been taken to signal that after devolution and the establishment of a Scottish Parliament in 1999, local political problems are over, and a newly enlivened national culture can compete normally again in the worldwide literary marketplace. This reading has become a way of avoiding noticing that the concerns of Kelman's Glasgow fiction are more forcefully rearticulated in global terms – a repositioning most visible in *Translated Accounts*, which, while retaining many of the earlier themes, makes itself impossible to identify and market as 'ethnically' Scottish, using an anonymous political landscape which evokes a range of peripheral, neocolonial or semi-occupied regions. Reading this demands a general rethinking of the periphery – where this term refers to comparable forms outside a core tradition – and also has a special significance for 'English', since 'English' tends to shift between denoting place, language and literary discourse, and, although somehow central to the tone of the field, is finally indefinable. 'English' denotes not only a language but also a core authority based on linguistic *absence*, in a perfect analogue of the way power is derived from the unwritten constitution. So one contest taking place in world English is between writing on one hand which is active and causes redefinition of the self's place in society, and on the other an undeclared core power which does not belong to any specific place, functions as activity rather than action, and sees writing merely as a reflection of speech. The impulse of core culture, the authority based on absence, will always be to make peripheral writing *visible* and therefore easier to place; it will want to see the world's literary Englishes as non-comparable, specific and ethnic, and even, as refusing English altogether.

So while there is little linguistic justification for describing Kelman as resisting English, since his work contains a wide spectrum of English, including Standard English (SE), since English must be conceived by the core culture as something which is not active, there is a strong tendency to identify him with 'anti-English' linguistic politics – compounded by frequent descriptions of his writing as 'speech' (see Chapter 8). This tendency – familiar in criticism of postcolonial and third world literature – is especially common amongst sympathetic critics. Nicola Pitchford, for example, reads Cairns Craig's description of *How late* as showing 'a manipulation of narrative point of view to *insist upon* the spoken language of Sammy and his peers, not only by reproducing that language but by making it the exclusive language of narration.'[10] The question this begs is why non-SE narration is accepted as being more speech-based than SE narration. Are non-SE dialects spoken before they are written, and is non-SE writing then merely 'reproducing language'? The idea that writing is simply a reflection of speech – and that there are 'vernacular' languages which are somehow not textual – denies peripheral fiction access to much of the literary thought of the last half-century or so, in which writing has specific properties and is powerful for what it does *as writing*. Since much of this thought is French and threatens the way that tradition must remain ungraspable by writing, this is exactly the kind of connection that core English is keen to block. But on the contrary, writing at the periphery tends to be *less* directly mimetic, and more highly structured and estranged; there tends to be more literary artifice and less realism, making it less rather than more directly dependent on speech.[11] Kelman's Glasgow fiction sets the tone, and an extreme version of free indirect discourse allows the voice of the narrator to bleed into the voice of the character, making classical realist perspectives hard to stabilise (see Chapter 3), and undermining ways in which core English naturalises experience. The unwillingness to 'perspectivise' narration also makes difficult the packaging of ethnic difference for global literary markets, in which there is a constant, core-driven demand for vernacular.[12]

In different forms, the negotiations caused by the pressure of the demand for ethnic authenticity are familiar to regions struggling (or failing) to emerge from colonialism. For Salman Rushdie post-imperial narrative is characterised by a negotiation between high and low voices designed to remain unplaceable in ethnic terms.[13] This restlessness typifies, according to Elleke Boehmer, a period of 'crossing, fragmenting, and parodying', particularly in Indo-Anglian fiction. In the tradition of Shashi Tharoor's *The Great Indian Novel* and Rushdie's own *Midnight's Children*,

> local contexts are reflected in inclusion of pidgin English, in translated words, obscure proverbs. The writer introduces a noise of voices that resist easy

decoding. A similar effect is created where a work cites cultural information
– jokes, fragments of oral epic, indigenous film, vernacular histories – which
cannot be deciphered without background knowledge.[14]

An insistence on local terms, idioms, artifacts and scraps of music describes
the kind of textual resistance built up by fragments of writing in the Glasgow-
based Kelman. It is not that the contexts are innately more or less difficult
than SE, but that they are not easy to 'broker' by translation into SE for global
markets:

> Chic kept on walking, shoulders hunched into the wind, on round the corner.
> There were four pubs in the immediate vicinity but there were drawbacks to
> each; two of them just boring but the other two were no-go areas, sectarian dis-
> asters, prehistoric politics, the way ye asked for a pint left a mark on yer fucking
> foreheid. And Chic was moving to enter the first yin, the nearest yin. What did
> it matter, I couldnay be bothered stopping him. He led the way to the bar. A
> cunt was lying on the pool table out-the-game, fucking comatose. It was a thing
> no to notice.[15]

To be sure, Kelman's localised Glasgow fiction does not easily map on to
the mode of colonial fiction which portrays the disruption of a native culture
by occupation, as in many writers influenced by Chinua Achebe. Ismail Talib
rightly points out that Achebe's cross-translation between languages, and
between established and colloquial forms, can be seen as a general pattern
in postcolonial writing.[16] While Kelman's 'vernacularity' fits this pattern up
to a point, he departs from the insistence on the integrity of a 'native' form.
Unlike Achebe's African Trilogy, there is little interest in reconstructing
a discrete 'native' worldview; rather, there is an already globalised cultural
struggle from which there is no ideal escape, in which English offers the move
to a lingua franca while simultaneously concretising social class.

A stronger analogue exists in the Caribbean fiction of the mid-1950s to the
mid-1970s – that is, the period just before the 1980s Scottish literary renaissance. One reason for the relevance of this Caribbean writing to the Scottish
fiction of the period of Kelman's emergence is its relatively centreless model
of linguistic authority. Multiple possibilities within English are describable
less in terms of discrete languages or dialects, than in terms of a 'creole
continuum', in which there are sliding ranges of linguistic possibilities. The
continuum enables, or rather forces, a constant choice between forms, elic-
iting a dialectical movement. Rather than either fixing on a pre-existing
standard or fetishising an ideal native language, the continuum insists on a
continuous performance of linguistic choice. The term 'performance' is key,
since the *performative* form of the nation disturbs the pre-existing or 'anterior'
form which is taken for granted and which tends to take an ideal ethnic

form; linguistic 'performance' is precisely what the UK constitution avoids in remaining unwritten. The creole continuum means that tradition has a different and less stabilising function; it is no longer a question of accepting or rejecting English, but of 'code-switching' through the many class-inflected and nuanced possibilities open to people who speak at least two dialects – a prominent feature of post-1979 Scottish fiction.

One especially relevant Caribbean model is to be found in the work of Sam Selvon. His best-known work, *The Lonely Londoners* (1956), comprises Kelman-like tales of street-wandering and bedsit-living by recent Caribbean migrants to the metropolis. Selvon not only employs marked lexical differences from SE and neologism, he also presents SE and non-SE grammars as *choices* available to his narrator: for example, in idiom ('It was' for 'There was'), tense ('He come' for 'He came'). Characters show a strong degree of verbal awareness in manipulating dialect according to the needs of the situation, and their negotiation of SE is a key method of characterisation. Galahad, for example, seems to fall into linguistic traps just as he falls into the traps of London life, especially when he 'corrects' his speech beyond the level of the literary narration:

> 'Mummy, look at that black man!' A little child, holding on to the mother hand, look up at Sir Galahad.
> 'You mustn't say that, dear!' The mother chide the child.
> But Galahad's skin like rubber at this stage, he bend don and pat the child cheek, and the child cower and shrink and begin to cry.
> 'What a sweet child!' Galahad say, putting on the old English accent, 'What's your name?'
> But the child mother uneasy as they stand up there on the pavement with so many white people around: if they was alone she might have talked a little, and ask Galahad what part of the world he come from, but instead she pull the child along and she look at Galahad and give a sickly sort of smile, and the old Galahad, knowing how it is, smile back and walk on.[17]

As in one of Kelman's tales of tense urban silence, the full meaning of this encounter is revealed via subjunctive possibility ('if they was alone'), rendered in a particularised language signalling *invisible* difference, a migrant subjectivity which eludes the racial gaze. Kelman's identity as a writer has far more to do with such affiliations across peripheries than nativist belonging: similarity to 'where' rather than a common 'who'. He is continually drawn to writers responding to analogous political-linguistic pressures, rather than campaigning for the unique speech of a defined in-group. Casanova is right to allude to 'a strange dialectic, which authors on the periphery alone understand' – but Kelman is difficult to club as a member of the international brigade of exotic marginals in a multicultural market.

The model of minor literature discerned in Franz Kafka by Gilles Deleuze and Félix Guattari offers another account of the relation between literary cores and peripheries. A way of describing the work of peripheral literatures in a core language, the minor does not just refer to an individual author's dialect – as is frequently claimed by its detractors – but also more generally to the potential to create new literary forms below the level of the state, which is where Casanova sometimes comes unstuck. Non-standard language can *perform* the national in terms of its misfit with state culture, and move away from the 'vehicular language' which is an 'urban, even worldwide language, a language of business, commercial exchange, bureaucratic transmission'.[18]

The move from *How late* to *Translated Accounts* illustrates this, since the former novel sets out a specific type of place-inflected experience, and the latter demonstrates how the difficulty of negotiating a vehicular language is a general one. Drew Milne stresses that in this, rather than the writer's own idiolect, lies the importance of the minor:

> it hardly seems to matter that the corrupted discourses of power in *The Trial* might reflect no specifically German and Czech questions of language [. . .] *Translated Accounts* reinvents the Kafkaesque with sinister authorities and bureaucratic brutality as an almost comic, everyday kind of alienation.[19]

So in Kelman, as in Kafka, a struggle with the core language is associated with a struggle with the form of the state. In *How late*, as in *The Trial*, Sammy is co-opted into talking by agencies which he knows will use his speech against him, as well as by a state shill who mediates and regulates his language.[20] *How late* also recalls Kafka's 'The Metamorphosis' in having Sammy wake up as a different kind of creature, one forced to recreate or 'world' his environment in terms of its physical immediacy. This move towards the tactile is a postcolonial one, since empire has operated by extending power in terms of space and visual categorisation, and viewed, quantified and categorised in terms of the idea of 'race' – where Sam Selvon's 'Look at that black man!', is close to the description of the appearance of the racial gaze in Frantz Fanon. The struggle to escape this kind of placement is the struggle to escape state ideology, which works through official 'vehicular' language; experience is kept out of touch, universal and impersonal. This pattern is given specific historical grounding in Kelman's fiction; Sammy's anxiety about being watched matches a rapid rise in public surveillance cameras, first piloted for street use in Scotland in the mid-1980s.[21] Being perpetually observed necessitates the evasive movement of code-switching – a dialectical movement – which, since it is not simply oppositional, avoids, as Simon Baker puts it, 'the circumscribing trap of showing characters battling against an immovable system, because such resistance is implicit in the disruptive literary gesture itself.'[22]

Told in snatches of mutilated 'found' prose, the stage of *Translated Accounts* is pointedly non-specific, shifting from descriptions evoking the Niger Delta to scenes resembling the Middle East; the territory of the novel is a highly politicised non-place. Refusing the linguistic authority of an ethnic 'here', its language, as Susanne Hagemann says, 'belongs to nobody', and so any naturalising force of a core language becomes impossible – a 'distancing' method Hagemann rightly compares to Russian Formalism (see Chapter 8).[23] The book is also, though, noticeably aligned with the literature of Nigeria, a neocolonial regime using English as a lingua franca, challenged by the 'counter-anthropological', nativist tradition of fiction following Achebe. If the Caribbean is the first, Nigeria is the second major zone of affinity for Kelman's English. An influence of particular importance is Amos Tutuola's *The Palm-Wine Drinkard* (1952), a novel seen with as much suspicion by well-to-do Nigerians as *How late* was by well-to-do Scots. As Kelman says in his 1997 obituary of Tutuola, 'it isn't surprising that this kinship should exist between writers [Amos Tutuola and Sam Selvon] engaged in similar formal struggles. What is so striking is that the context should remain unfathomable to the mainstream world of English literature.'[24]

Tutuola's method is a restructuring of English from below which came to be known in the early 1970s as 'inter-language', a term 'used to characterize the genuine and discrete linguistic system employed by learners of a second language.'[25] Functioning as an 'approximate system', inter-language displays a range of non-standard grammatical and syntactic forms, as in this extract from *The Palm-Wine Drinkard*:

> Then I started to find out another expert palm-wine tapster, but I could not get me one who could tap the palm-wine to my requirement. When there was no palm-wine for me to drink I started to drink ordinary water which I was unable to taste before, but I did not satisfy with it as palm-wine.[26]

It is a learner-esque English packed with officialese, but which is none the less shown to have achieved a degree of autonomous expressive authority.[27] For Bill Ashcroft et al., Tutuola's inter-language is 'paradigmatic of all cross-cultural writing, since the development of a creative language is not a striving for competence in the dominant tongue, but a striving towards appropriation, in which the cultural distinctiveness can be simultaneously overridden-overwritten.'[28] It is in precisely this sense that Kelman hails Tutuola as 'a tradition-bearer in an alien language'.[29] The wider implication is that those outside of the core 'learn' SE as a remote dialect of power. The inter-language is not 'Scots' (a nativist model), but rather a kind of 'broken English' along Tutuola's model, and the struggle to occupy non-Standard English as a literary form.

The violent relationship between broken and 'whole' English is thematised by Tutuola's fellow Nigerian Ken Saro-Wiwa, especially in *Sozaboy* (1985), where power is associated with 'big grammar', good standing and the ability to defend oneself.[30] Literary inter-language critiques the way linguistic violence is linked to physical violence, forcing silence in the face of authority:

> The man with fine shirt stood up. And began to talk in English. Big big words. Grammar. 'Fantastic. Overwhelming. Generally. In particular and in general'. Haba, God no go vex. But he did not stop there. The big grammar continued. 'Odious. Destruction. Fighting'. I understand that one. 'Henceforth. General mobilization. All citizens. Able-bodied. Join the military. His Excellency. Powers conferred on us. Conscription'. Big big words. Long long grammar. 'Ten heads. Vandals. Enemy.' Everybody was silent.[31]

The Nigerian question is how to make the lived language literary without resorting to ideal expressions of difference. If Salman Rushdie insists English is an Indian language in the modern Indo-Anglian tradition, and Caribbean writers including George Lamming have stressed how English is a West Indian language, so *Translated Accounts* depicts the struggle for agency by code-switching between imaginary peripheries which have all been battered by a global system of commodified language.[32] Kelman's refusal of ethnic specificity also prevents the Romantic spectacle of a native language rising up 'against' English only to reaffirm English in its difference – and the refusal of a saleable ethnic form like 'Scots language' is doubtless one reason the book was so badly received by both Scottish brokers of ethnicity and the multicultural-statist wing of the British press. By the time of *You Have to be Careful*, Kelman's narrator is out to mock 'native' Scottish forms ('What is "ach" in pictish?') even while he links the linguistic to the active to the national: '[actors in my film] would all need a good Skarrish tongue in their heid [. . .] And nayn of that shite where they tone it down for the worldwide bourgeois language markets'.[33]

The fact that the (neo)colonial Nigerian state so closely took the shape of capital, rather than staying responsive to national form, is significant for the post-1979 Scottish literary renaissance. The spectral presences in *The Palm-Wine Drinkard*, for example – ghosts of other possible voices – are cited in the 'Index of Plagiarisms' in Alasdair Gray's *Lanark* (the entry on Tutuola ends 'see also KAFKA').[34] These neo-Gothic presences also appear in the 'spectral body' chapter of *Translated Accounts* and in the mysterious 'apparitional' figure known as the 'Being' in *You Have to be Careful* (the Being is 'not to be gazed upon' and seems undetectable even by CCTV).[35] As *How late* embeds its dialectic within a critique of the surveillant UK state, so *Translated Accounts* laces its inter-language with cryptic references to Saro-Wiwa's struggle against the oil giant Shell, whose practices he described as financially and ecologically disastrous (and comparisons could be made with the UK exploitation of North Sea oil).[36] Saro-Wiwa's arrest and imprisonment by the Nigerian authorities in 1993-4 prompted both emergency moves to rouse international leaders and widespread protests from the literary world, including a letter from Achebe, Harold Pinter, Susan Sontag and others objecting to abuse by 'security officers [. . .] and military guards' reminiscent of *Translated Accounts*.[37] Saro-Wiwa's trial speech, like the hyper-mediated vehicular English of *Translated Accounts*, reveals the managerial, cultural and bureaucratic cast behind state power: 'The military do not act alone. They are supported by a gaggle of politicians, lawyers, academics and businessmen.'[38] So in *Translated Accounts* state power encourages an 'official politics' − 'practical formalities that were not politics' − which trivialises debate by making it seem like ethnic conflict − a position strongly resisted by Saro-Wiwa, who says in *Prisoners of Jebs*: 'on the surface, it may appear I have been making an argument for the Ogoni project. But in essence, I have been questioning the entire Nigerian system.'[39] *Translated Accounts* highlights the danger which attends the revelation of apparently ethnic protest as general peripheral political critique. The encounter with core power underscores the vulnerability of small peripheral groups to surveillance when they join to address the generalised power of the state:

> Colleagues established contact with people of outer communities, leaders there, tinier pressure groups, tinier campaigns in tinier townships, little little villages. These were distrustful, that the involvement of our 'campaigning formation' would bring to them trouble from securitys or military. It so was for them, and so would be.[40]

The stilted but 'intact' SE hints at the fragility of the common bond achieved by such chains of association. The section entitled 'a pumpkin story' turns to the channels and conduits which *connect* peripheral organisations. Connoting the pollution of the Niger Delta by oil waste, here pipelines contaminate rivers at the level of language:

> Water and oil, these are international. Rivers may be pipes. I have heard them so called. [. . .] People do not say oil-river, rivers are of water, water gives life but of a water-river people may say of it it is a pipe. [. . .] If water is sealed off from people what is it, it is a pipe. [. . .] Foreign lands have rivers, all have pipes, pipes are crossing borders, international.[41]

As the corrupted SE of the novel violates any ideal of organic language, nature stops being a normalising force in sentences which themselves seem unnatural, and have the paratactic 'listing' tendency of the language of someone prevented from making wider connections. Achebe once famously insisted that English should be remade rather than lost 'as a means of international exchange'[42] – but for the figures we half-discern in *Translated Accounts*, globalisation creates a perpetually uneven exchange. Capital flows not from linguistic competence, but from linguistic ignorance; the existence of the story itself assumes an ability in English as a learned language, but the managerial overclass rest on *prior* authority and so deny the action of language in creating shared experience:

> What language could he know. There is a language shared, man to man, with woman, why he did not leave, and watched us, myself, what did he think, why he was there watching us. He knows, man knows. He was there. Thinking I so am foolish we are so foolish. Why? I do not go to his country.[43]

In this 'generalised' state of alienation, there is even a dedicated space for ethnic fantasies of homecoming – the airport.[44] This becomes the central stage of *You Have to be Careful in the Land of the Free*, narrated by a Scottish soldier drafted into the security industry, and defending organised capital in an airport which doubles as a detention camp, where passengers are joined by homeless gamblers pushing their possessions around in shopping trolleys, as if lost in the global marketplace. Like *How late*, the novel uses an extreme version of free indirect discourse – now in first person – to collapse realist perspective, and like *Translated Accounts*, expression rises up through the lingua franca of consumers' English discarded by others on their trajectories through the airport. The novel's idiomatic surrealism forbids paraphrase ('Every bit of the essential detail we need to bulk out a fantasy, all of it was there'[45]) but strongly evokes the political mobilisation of anti-realism in the post-war Caribbean, where vernacular writing was explicitly linked to an aesthetic of national resistance.[46] The link between the national and the desire to interfere with the apparent transparency of referential language has a high point in surrealism, and is also seen, for example, in Edward Kamau Brathwaite's *nation language* as 'an English which is not the standard, imported, educated English, but that of submerged, surrealist experience and sensibility, which has always been there and is now increasingly coming to the surface.'[47]

Caribbean surrealist language in fact has a close historical relationship with Scottish literature of the 1960s onwards, and Kelman's background is slightly misrepresented by Casanova's grouping him with Tom Leonard, as a ready-made school close in terms of age and interest in the vernacular – missing the proximity to the key formal innovator of the period, Edwin Morgan. The coalescence tends to go deep into Scottish modernism. Contra the Anglo-British organic ideal, the literary history of modernism shows that economic conflicts at the periphery tend to lead to formal experiment that only slowly is managed into the core.[48] In this sense, there is a way of looking at Kelman, especially the early 2000s Kelman, which is less about fitting the work into a central modernist tradition, than about seeing the ways in which literary modernism is itself identifiable in terms of its problematic relationship with centres and traditions.

CHAPTER TEN

Kelman and Masculinity

Carole Jones

> He had fucking reached it now man the fucking dregs man the pits, the fucking
> black fucking limboland, purgatory; that's what it was like, purgatory, where all
> ye can do is think.
>
> *How late it was, how late*[1]

If James Kelman's fiction has one enduring subject, it is the masculine condition in the contemporary period. At the centre of his work is the solitary
male figure for whom existence is a perplexing challenge to physical, spiritual
and psychic well-being. Despite the unheroic lives of his male characters,
Kelman is often grouped with other Scottish male authors, such as William
McIlvanney, Irvine Welsh and Ian Rankin, who write from an overarching
male point of view and whose works are often dominated by the hyper-
masculinised 'hard man'. Neil McMillan asserts that along with these others
Kelman produces texts which 'fail to question their own residual masculinism': that is, their habit of promoting styles, values and ways of knowing
which privilege men and masculinity.[2] Kelman's writing, from this perspective, joins a 'representational pact' in contemporary Scottish fiction identified by Christopher Whyte, in which the prevalence of the hard man signals
that 'the task of embodying and transmitting Scottishness is, as it were,
devolved to the unemployed, the socially underprivileged', due to the greater
authenticity of their Scottishness in speech and social practice.[3] Indeed,
Kelman's characterisation of writing as a type of guerrilla class warfare evokes
the aggressive masculinity Whyte has in mind. In the 2007 'Afterword' to *An
Old Pub Near the Angel*, Kelman repeated his argument that a writer needs to
find ways 'to hijack third-person narrative from the voice of imperial authority'; writing is a 'weapon', a response to a situation analogous to 'somebody
punching the fuck out ye [. . .] but ye went away and attended the cuts,
had a shower, and came back with Daddy's axe'.[4] Such emotive statements
– casting the novel as a militarised war-zone – tend to bolster Kelman's
reputation as a hard man writer.

Kelman's male characters are far more complex, uncertain and vulnerable than this stereotype allows. His protagonists are typically disempowered men who react by retreating into themselves; Kelman's male narratives are about self-doubt, stasis and paralysis, leavened with spare but persistent humour. While his use of working-class protagonists and the Glasgow vernacular allows antagonistic critics to dismiss his fiction as coarse 'literary vandalism', his anxious portraits of men in crisis present them not as aggressors but as victims.[5] There are contradictory political currents in this portrayal which make male identity a crucial site of conflict in Kelman's writing.

The key model of male identity in Kelman's fiction is described by Sammy Samuels in How late it was, how late: 'purgatory, where all ye can do is think'.[6] The introspective or 'thinking' subject, gazing inwardly at his own consciousness, is a particularly masculine model of selfhood, being autonomous and removed from the world and others, and suggesting a radical separateness of mind and body. This binary relation represents men's traditionally privileged access to reason as set against women's association with the material realm of bodily experience. But why should this introspective condition be linked to the Catholic notion of 'purgatory', that third state, neither Heaven nor Hell, in which souls adjudged to be neither damned nor free of sin endure a painful wait for purification? This complex image suggests that the identity of the self-perceiving thinker is more a matter of faith than fact, and that even the privacy of the inner life is shaped by powerful cultural constructs from 'outside' the self. Patriarchal masculinity establishes its hegemony, argues R. W. Connell, partly by its 'claim to embody the power of reason', by spurning the body and its corollaries of emotion and feeling, and seeking transcendence over and control of material reality.[7] For Kelman, however, the male condition is not power over the world but existential suffering in it, a realisation of powerlessness, uncertainty and a radical instability of selfhood. From this angle, the purgatorial image may be read as a critique of inherited notions of masculinity, in which the cogito, the Cartesian 'I think therefore I am,' has been a privileged model. This chapter aims to show how Kelman's portrayal of masculinity challenges and deeply problematises dominant conceptions of male identity, to the point of conjuring its disappearance.

Purgatory is a borderland between death and redemption, a marginal condition like that constantly enacted in the forms and patterns of Kelman's writing. The anxious repetitions and tense silence of his characters suggest both restlessness and paralysis ('all ye can do is think'), compulsive mental pacing around no-man's-land:

Aw christ he was tired. How the hell could he no just drop off! just fucking drop off. It was his back, it was sore, he couldnay lie on his front cause of the bracelets and he couldnay get comfy he just couldnay get fucking comfy, know what I'm talking about fucking comfy, comfy fucking comfy he was fucking fuckt man he was fuckt, that's what he was, fuckt, fucking bastarn good night, good fucking night, if he could sleep, if he could just sleep; but how the fuck can ye sleep if ye cannay get comfy? It's a straight question.[8]

This writing traces and re-traces the limits of masculinity, questioning what it is to be a man, and drawing attention to the instability and weakly secured boundaries of male identity.

Kelman's preoccupation with margins relates to his concern to write from the position of the 'other', and to give voice to those not represented in dominant discourse. He consistently frames his work as liberatory, as writing 'that nobody else is going to be oppressed by',[9] located as 'part of a much wider process, or movement, toward decolonization and self-determination'.[10] However, the oppressed other here is insistently male. Does Kelman 'appropriate' victim status for men, as a means of re-securing and re-establishing male authority?[11] Ben Knights has observed that the helplessness and dependency of Kelman's male characters can be read as emasculating; their 'appeals to sympathy [are] usurping a conventionally feminine position' which 'amounts to a perverse kind of claim to centrality'.[12] McMillan also perceives Kelman's strategy as 'locating his characters in ideologically feminine spaces of interiority, passivity and pathos.'[13] These interpretations perceive a reasserting or re-centring of male dominance and even of a phallic or patriarchal authority in Kelman's writing: his 'hard style', as McMillan terms it.

On the other hand, the weakness and disempowerment of Kelman's men can be read as *resistance* to a hegemonic identity in which strength, control, autonomy, agency and stability are the privileged signifiers of male dominance.[14] In Kelman's novels we see a gradual movement away from this model. The status of the central male character, for example, moves from relative nearness to the discursive centre of male power, toward its margins. The hero of *The Busconductor Hines* fits an archetype of working-class fiction: a family man, married with a young son, endeavouring to hold on to his job. In *A Disaffection*, Patrick Doyle is single, a sexual failure, and trying to lose his job as a teacher. In *How late*, Sammy is an outsider, an unemployed construction worker who has lost his girlfriend and his eyesight. Both *Translated Accounts* and *You Have to be Careful in the Land of the Free* radically undercut characters' autonomy and stability; the former is organised around the disembodied voices of the displaced and persecuted, while the hero of the latter, Jeremiah Brown, is an immigrant far from home, a father estranged from his child and former partner. As an 'unassimilatit alien', a wanderer without a legitimate place, Jeremiah is reduced to working for 'the wage of an adolescent'.[15] Most recently, *Kieron Smith, boy* follows the life of a young Glaswegian from the age of about four to twelve; here the faraway shore of masculine freedom and responsibility is glimpsed only fleetingly through his grandfather and father.

This sequence of novels traces a gradual shift away from assertive, recognised masculinity, and a sustained exploration of masculinity as a *produced* identity, via textual strategies which dramatise the enactment and policing of male subjectivity. Failure, crisis and unease loom large. *A Disaffection* opens with the lines: 'Patrick Doyle was a teacher. Gradually he had become sickened by it.'[16] At the beginning of *How late* Sammy is waking from a stupor on the street, and almost immediately reflects 'there's something far far wrong; ye're no a good man, ye're just no a good man.'[17] Early in *You Have to be Careful in the Land of the Free* Jeremiah portrays himself in similar terms:

> I was an ex Security operative, how Uhmerkin can ye get! Okay, failed Security operative. No really a failure, I just didnay make a career out it. But add to that failed husband and failed parent, failed father, general no fucking hoper. And now I was gaun hame, gaun hame! I was a failed fucking immigrant![18]

This powerful sense of inadequacy extends even unto 'the fucking black fucking limboland, purgatory' of the inner life.[19] These men verge on hysteria, that particularly feminised loss of control of rational power over self and environment.[20] Kelman's treatment of the male *body* is of particular interest in this context. Scott Hames describes Kelman's narrative subjects as 'leaky' and 'exercis[ing] less control over their own boundaries' than is traditionally expected of men.[21] As Jane Gallop writes in *Thinking Through the Body*, 'men have their masculine identity to gain by being estranged from their bodies and dominating the bodies of others.'[22] For Margrit Shildrick, this estrangement relies on securing the boundaries of the body in contrast to the traditionally conceived situation of women:

> Women, unlike the self-contained and self-containing men, leaked; or, as [Elisabeth] Grosz claims: 'women's corporeality is inscribed as a mode of seepage'. The issue throughout Western cultural history has been one of female lack of closure [. . .] The indeterminacy of body boundaries challenges that most fundamental dichotomy between self and other, unsettling ontological certainty and threatening to undermine the basis on which the knowing self establishes control.[23]

We can read Kelman's primary textual strategies in light of such threats to autonomy and stability.

The dramatised self-consciousness common to Kelman's fiction does suggest estrangement from the body and its limitations. As Hames points out, 'if [Kelman's protagonists] are enslaved by objective circumstances, they are unchallenged masters of the interior reality to which they escape,' a mode of representation coded to promote a 'practice of self-mastery [. . .] which affirms the self-presence of the ego and raises its transparency to the status of "objective" self-control.'[24] Hames immediately dismisses this possibility, however, asserting that Kelman's men 'are never permitted these consolations of self-mastery', tormented as they are 'by the disorder of their inner worlds, and their *lack* of rational self-discipline'.[25] Such an argument continues to promote the idea of a masculine estrangement from the body. However, it is not simply their inner disorder that undermines men here. The constant interruption of the body in these texts – the ongoing references to its presence and effects which appear to disturb the narration from its course – undermines that estrangement, counters any occasion for self-aggrandisement, and actualises the threat to autonomy, stability and 'ontological certainty' identified by Shildrick. If we revisit Sammy's 'comfy' lament quoted above, we can see the connection between Sammy's bodily and psychological security. In that passage he is verging on hysteria, incapable of controlling his actions, even when his only desire is to sleep, to lose consciousness and give up control. The body is his barrier to oblivion, frustrating his desire, but also demonstrating his inability to escape or transcend the material realm.

Bodily appetites, needs and addictions repeatedly call attention to the material status of Kelman's men (particularly smoking). The interruption of the body is, at crucial times, insistently physical. The section of Sammy's 'comfy' lament in *How late*, for instance, concludes with the sentence, 'Fucking pong as well, the phantom fucking farter man he was at it again,' in reference to the man sharing Sammy's police cell.[26] Crying is a more conventional test of masculine control, both emotional and physical. In the moment Rab Hines returns to his flat to discover his wife has apparently left him, 'he sat down on the armchair and started to greet. It was a strange thing. His face didnt alter and nor did his eyes redden, and he stopped it right away.'[27] Sammy, emotionally roused by a song, belatedly realises 'There was tears coming out, he fucking felt them.'[28] The action or event of crying is brought to our attention here, not the emotions being experienced – Sammy 'felt them' as *physical* phenomena. This disconnection between mind and body contrasts sharply with the reader's direct proximity to Sammy's mental life, and suggests a profound internal alienation.

The more necessary and natural breaching of bodily boundaries – calls of nature – can also create an acute sense of anxiety. The opening of *A Disaffection* has Patrick 'round the back of the premises for a pish'; just why he feels the need to do this in isolation outside the 'local arts centre' is not explained.[29] Jeremiah in *You Have to be Careful* needs to urinate for most of the novel. He spends the second half of the text at bursting-point and the close of the narrative finds him in a dark, snowy suburban landscape still not having relieved himself. We leave him in that state of urinary distress which was signalled over 200 pages before when, sitting by himself in a bar, he resists having to get up and go to the toilet in case he loses his seat: 'Aw dear, nay option, safeguard the bladder. Naw! Fuck the "aw dear, nay option, safeguard the bladder" shite, I wasnay gauny be dictated to by any body, no even my ayn. I would exercise mind ower matter.'[30] There is knowing humour in Jeremiah's stubborn resistance to the demands of 'matter', but elsewhere in Kelman's work we see male characters imagining a kind of pleasurable surrender to bodily weakness ('If the truth be told I was fond of my physical ailments').[31] Hines's fantasy of physical obliteration is closely linked to maternal imagery:

> He bit a large mouthful of the bread, and cheese, as though by blocking his mouth and respiratory system his digestive system would be forced into taking action; he sipped the tea to aid its progress. O christ he felt like chucking it. A good greet could solve everything. She [his mother] would settle his head against her breasts, pat his back rhythmically, crooning an auld scotch sang till he toppled off the edge to go crashing on the jaggy boulders below. A mother's love is that which is required. Thrust me back in out the road for fuck sake mammy I need to hide away, away.[32]

The depth of Hines's feminising resignation is indexed by this complete breakdown of physical self-command; even the involuntary, 'automatic' bodily systems resist his will, and ingenious mental stratagems are required to 'force' it into 'action'. The privileged cornerstones of male identity, autonomy and action, are renounced together as Hines yearns for the sanctuary of the womb.

That emblems of the feminine are so prominent in this desire for disappearance signals some difficult issues relating to Kelman's representation of women, for which he has been criticised.[33] We never have privileged access to a female consciousness in Kelman's work, but when women do appear, they are – from the perspectives of his male characters – strong, in control and often powerful. But gender intersects with class in Kelman's work. With this in mind, Neil McMillan suggests another dimension to the political significance of Kelman's women, situating his work within a pattern of Scottish working-class writing stretching back to the 1930s:

> In the specific ideological ensemble which makes up Kelman's work, the 'other' space which women occupy is also consistently identified as bourgeois. Alison and Sandra, like most of the women in the earlier Glasgow novels, are middle class, or at least upwardly mobile [. . .] Kelman persistently identifies womanliness with negative bourgeois aspirations.[34]

Certainly women like Hines's wife Sandra demonstrate such aspirations for conventional success, expressed in the desire to move to a better area, acquire a better job, and live a more comfortable, affluent life.[35]

This association with discredited 'male' ambition, however, is tempered by Kelman women who responsibly keep men's feet on the ground, regulating their linguistic and emotional excess. Towards the end of *A Disaffection* a tipsy Patrick's need to engage his sister-in-law Nicola in conversation is thwarted by her resistance to his gushing sentimentality. In reply to his misty-eyed view of his four-year-old niece (as having 'a real sense of peace' compared to her brother), Nicola insists that 'Women have to listen more than men, that's why they've got a sense of peace as you call it.' She goes on, 'I'm not criticising you Pat but I think you've got a glamourised view of women which is wrong, it really is wrong.'[36] When Patrick conjures up the beautiful view from the top of the Red Road flats, she counters:

> The Red Road flats is an awful place to live. When I was at school in Balornock I had a friend and she had a cousin living there and her mother killed herself.
> Pat was about to say something but he stopped.[37]

Sentimentalism is not the only concern; language and its responsible use is a preoccupation of Kelman's women, who often disapprove of men swearing, and encourage children (such as Kieron Smith) to speak 'properly'. This is not mere conformism; women's verbal caution contrasts with a male linguistic incontinence which often leads to trouble. In *How late* Sammy describes his partner Helen as 'good at silence',[38] a characteristic shared with Yasmin in *You Have to be Careful*: 'What did Yasmin say? Fuck all. She listened.'[39] There is a sense here of stronger, stiffer, more stable personal boundaries in women: of greater autonomy and self-control. Simon Kövesi asks whether these consistent feminine strengths reflect Kelman's own 'glamourised view of women'.[40] Perhaps it is not a view of 'women' at all; what these texts position as attractive and admirable in women are qualities traditionally associated with *masculinity*. Can we go further than Kövesi, then, and ask whether Kelman's cautious and slightly awed reverence towards his female characters amounts to a strategy of re-routing hegemonic masculinity through women?

Women are not strangers to power in Kelman's fiction; 'Ye meet them everywhere too in these official capacities,' says Sammy in reference to the woman who interviews him at the benefit office in *How late*.[41] She emanates a 'sensation of total and absolute fucking cleanliness man [. . .] class or something'.[42] Though he is blind he can imagine her:

> Sammy knew this kind of woman. Totally beautiful in a weird way; didnay matter what like she was, her build, nothing. Dead sexual as well. Sometimes they wear these smart-cut suits, their blouses are low-cut and they're beautiful and ye're at a total disadvantage.[43]

Sammy's sexualising of the woman's authority may be an attempt to diminish her status as an agent of the state, tracing her power to a traditional mystical and threatening femininity. But his translating of the class war into a battle of the sexes fails to achieve any self-vindicating conceptual power for him, and he is left 'fuckt', his disempowerment confirmed. Her ruthless interrogation, knowledge and control of the situation along with her invisible, ubiquitous presence – 'he hadnay heard her approach'[44] – signals her appropriation of masculinised authority.

In just this way, women in Kelman's fiction often serve to highlight the distance of his men from the dominant notions of hegemonic masculinity, their dwindling status and visibility in a world of masculinised power. Many of his protagonists, like Hines, express a desire to disappear which signals a resistance to both embodiment and assertive male identity. So of his newly experienced blindness, Sammy conjectures with guarded optimism, 'if this was permanent he wouldnay be able to see himself ever again. Christ that was wild. And he wouldnay see cunts looking at him. Wild right enough.'[45] And ending with the words 'that was him, out of sight,' *How late* enacts this disappearance.[46] Rather than a restatement of the traditional repression or ignoring of the male body in representation which serves to equate men with the mind and rationality, this resistance to visibility creates a contrast to the anxious, unstable, yet insistently present embodiment of Kelman's men. It signals a rejection of traditional models of male identity and their tendency to promote clearly delineated and essentialist explanations of male selfhood. These texts tentatively evoke a desire for new masculinities in a deliberate resistance to representation, an avoidance of defining and pinning down a singular notion of masculinity and its characteristics. Such a resistance is cap-tured in a distancing of material reality, in the conclusions of Kelman's later novels in particular, which succeeds in promoting a more complex approach to male subjectivity as a social construction, suggestively intimating that it is a production of social discourses often encountered and enabled in the fictions of everyday life.

This awareness of 'constructed' identity is palpable in the final section of *A Disaffection*, in which Patrick needlessly spins a yarn about being a shoemaker rather than a teacher, shortly before the fictive world becomes uncertain and menacing. In the final scenes, as Patrick runs away from police who may or may not be chasing him, and fantasises about revolutionary violence, he considers the temptation of suicide with reference to a biblical precedent: 'What is that story in the bible about a guy who commits suicide. [. . .] Who is that guy who commits suicide, as a thing to be committed.'[47] Jeremiah's last words refer to Billy the Kid, the beloved folk hero and outlaw. Male desire and aspiration appear to require translation through symbols and narrative, some repository of meaning outside the self, in order to be realised. At the end of *Kieron Smith, boy*, Kieron, who has a passion for dangerous climbing, fantasises about being saved from falling by his deceased grandfather's spirit:

> Maybe a bad spirit would make me do it. [. . .] if it was a ronepipe and ye were getting to the very top and the spirit just blew the wind and knocked ye off. So yer granda would be there, his spirit would come to yer rescue, maybe a breath of wind or a hard blowing wind, to stop ye hitting the ground heid first, ye would land one foot at a time, nice and soft, or else in a big pile of sacks and just get up and walk away, Oh that was lucky, and it would be, except if it was him, yer granda.[48]

These final words of the novel conjure a complex fantasy. Kieron mourns his dead grandfather, desires his transcendence of death, and yearns for the triumph of mind or spirit over body which is the enduring legacy of the ideal masculinity his grandfather embodies. This fantasy of disembodiment characterises the impossible desires of Kelman's protagonists, signalling the impossibility of masculinity itself, as traditionally conceived. It can be read as a recognition of the unreal nature of the heroic and hegemonic ideals embodied by Billy the Kid, Steve McQueen or Gary Cooper, but also as a sign of their ghostly, haunting residual presence.[49] Identity here is a fiction, achieved through the medium of fictions. In this altered perspective fantasy becomes the practical resource, rather than the cowardly refuge, of masculine identity. If Kelman's leaky narratives allow his men to slip from our grasp through the gaps – silences, contradictions and inarticulacies – of his texts, they open up possibilities for such fantasies of identity rather than closing them down in prescriptive ideals.

Kelman's fictions admit the pain and strangeness of embodiment for men and articulate a yearning for a *derealisation*, a dematerialisation of the male subject. Like these texts, his men are suspended between material reality and transcendence, in an 'other' space which is for some a feminised realm. However, the fragile stability of his embodied subjects prevents them from fully occupying any single position. Ultimately, Kelman's texts are on the border of masculinity, sometimes looking out from the inside of that border, sometimes on the outside looking in. His shimmying, oscillating representations produce yet resist weakness, produce yet resist identity, produce yet resist the material existence of the male body. Perhaps Jeremiah's urinary crisis is an exemplar of Kelman Man; he is left in a state of tension in the context of the imminent failure of his body's boundaries. He fails to find an appropriate receptacle, in Calvin Thomas's terms, for this bodily product, just as Kelman's men exceed the norms of male reason, analysis and self-consciousness.[50] This is not a comfortable state; as Sammy says, it is purgatory, suffering without the guarantee of relief. Kelman's writing of male anxiety marks him as an author resistant to preserving the boundaries of gendered identity and ego coherence, a writer who shares in Judith Butler's endeavour 'not to solve [. . .] the crisis of identity politics, but to proliferate and intensify this crisis [. . .] to affirm identity categories as a site of inevitable rifting.'[51] Kelman's literary riffing on the unstable boundaries of masculinity exposes, sustains and affirms that rifting.

CHAPTER ELEVEN

Kelman and the Existentialists

Laurence Nicoll

This chapter outlines some of the ways in which James Kelman's work both takes up and contributes to what he describes as the 'existentialist tradition'. Whilst the majority of the chapter will be concerned with an exploration of how Kelman's work can be usefully related to some existentialist forebears and some existentialist themes, it will also show that Kelman's avowed existentialism presents a number of difficulties and that these difficulties are produced by a disjunction between Kelman's open fictions and the closed world of his critical pronouncements. In short, whilst his novels and stories are carefully structured to resist definition and elude a certain type of judgement, his critical pieces do precisely the opposite. Invariably in the form of tendentious assertions, Kelman's dismissive attitude to other writers and to positions other than his own conflicts with precisely those existentialist notions of freedom that are vital to the production and comprehension of his fictions.

One of the great popularisers of existentialism, Walter Kaufmann, notes that the term is disowned by most of those to whom it is regularly applied. Additionally, attempts at a single definition of existentialism are invariably undone by the variety of thinkers and writers that the term is intended to encompass. Existentialism is, then, neither a settled school of thought nor reducible to a set of universal tenets. Kaufmann does, though, offer a definition based upon a common radicality. As a philosophy or philosophical approach, existentialism begins as a revolt against the philosophical establishment:

> The refusal to belong to any school of thought, the repudiation of the adequacy of any body of beliefs whatever, and especially of systems, and a marked dissatisfaction with traditional philosophy as superficial, academic, and remote from life – that is the heart of existentialism.[1]

This 'dissatisfaction', this concern that the traditional is somehow 'remote from life', underpins Kelman's critical work. When discussing the genesis of his writing, Kelman locates its foundations outside the mainstream English literary tradition. His first published interview, with Anne Stevenson in *The*

Scotsman, describes Katherine Anne Porter, Flannery O'Connor, Tillie Olsen and Sherwood Anderson as important models.[2] These writers are important because, as Kelman has it, they inhabit the margins of the established literary canon. Kelman's sense of artistic solidarity is not, though, simply a consequence of this perceived marginalisation; it is also based upon a shared conviction, an insistence, that the stories they write and the language they use are as valid as any other. These writers, and those discussed below, form, then, a counter-canon, a literary sourcebook, legitimating subjects and modes of writing Kelman finds lacking in the English mainstream. Kelman usefully elaborates upon his formative reading in the title essay of his collection *"And the judges said . . ."*:

> It was mainly American literature. Stories about pioneering communities, gamblers and rounders; boys who liked horses and wanted to be jockeys or newspapermen; tramps, cowboys, gangsters; small towns and big cities. All were rooted in a life that was recognisable, more or less, the lived-in, the everyday. [. . .] Equally significant for myself was a strain in European literature that asserted the primacy of the world as perceived and experienced by individual human beings. [. . .] So it was from an admixture of these two literary traditions, the European Existential and the American Realist, allied to British rock music, that I reached the age of twenty-two in the knowledge that certain rights were mine.[3]

Kelman's own aesthetic is the outcome of this 'admixture'. In Kelman's fictional work, existentialism and American realism interpenetrate and coalesce because both begin with, both examine and describe, the problematic everyday – the obstacles and trials of ordinary, unexceptional experience understood from the standpoint of, and narrated using the language of, the person in that situation. Attention to ordinary common incidents that comprise the diurnal reality of ordinary common people entails a literature with no extravagant plots, no grand progressive narratives where the poor orphan discovers that she is in fact an heiress. Instead, literature is built from, around and within small, applauseless, individual lives. Kelman, the American realists and the existentialists insist that there is enough in the everyday from which to create art and/or philosophy. Jean-Paul Sartre distinguishes between *le vécu* and *le connu*, between the lived and the known, with existentialism concerning itself entirely with the former. Yet, as Milan Kundera points out, the history of the novel is a history of engagement with precisely these philosophical, these 'living' problems: 'all the great existential themes Heidegger analyzes in *Being and Time* – considering them to have been neglected by all earlier European philosophy – have been unveiled, displayed, illuminated by four centuries of the novel.'[4] Literature engages with the existential when and where it clings to a life, a situation. The novel becomes existential when its themes become problems of and in a life: problems for some *one* in some *place*. Hence, for the existentialist, literature always has to be situated.

> Since we were *situated*, the only novels we could dream of were novels of *situation*, without internal narrators or all-knowing witnesses. In short if we wished to give an account of our age [. . .] we had to people our books with minds that were half lucid and half overcast, some of which we might consider with more sympathy than others, but none of which would have a privileged point of view either upon the event or upon itself. [. . .] We had to leave doubts, expectations, and the unachieved throughout our works, leaving it up to the reader to conjecture for himself by giving him the feeling, without giving him or letting him guess our feeling, that his view of the plot and the characters was merely one among many others.[5]

Sartre's position provides several pertinent points of illumination, for Kelman's fictions are also, clearly, 'novels of situation', of some one, in some place. Notice that Sartre's view of the situated text excludes the conventional third-person narrator or, indeed, any narrative position with a 'privileged' view. The conjunction of individual and situation must remain inviolate; existentialist texts are 'immanent', always positioned *within* the situation they depict. Kelman's narrative modes, whether they are second-person, third-person singular or, as with *You Have to be Careful in the Land of the Free*, first-person, are always narrated from within what they describe. Declining an omniscient narrative voice, the 'all-knowing witness' restores the ambiguity, the opaque quality, that is necessary to provide a sense that these events, this situation, is being undergone, is present, concrete, now. Actions and circumstances are, accordingly, presented without foretelling their outcome, without a sense that these events are already part of an established trajectory or narrative design. Outcomes must remain unknown not only for the narrator, but for the reader also; narrator, 'character' and reader must occupy the same plane. There are, as it were, no VIP seats.

A number of these issues are immediately apparent in *A Chancer*, but there are, too, some significant additions and extrapolations.[6] Structurally, the text is particulate, composed of discrete scenes. This almost atomistic construction is contiguous rather than continuous; each narrative segment bears little relation – temporally or spatially – to either that which precedes or that which ensues, rendering precisely the 'doubts' and sense of the unachieved that Sartre mentions above. This, along with the flat, sculpted, neutral quality of the prose, reveals Kelman's indebtedness to the work of Alain Robbe-Grillet, Nathalie Sarraute and the French 'New Novel', and also the influence of Albert Camus's *The Outsider*. Camus famously constructs his novel eschewing the past historic tense in favour of the perfect tense. This manœuvre, replacing, for example, 'I did' with 'I have done', might seem grammatically trivial but it carries enormous thematic significance for it signals a break with the grand narratives of the nineteenth-century realists, such as Balzac, and the associated notion that events unfold in a progressive determined manner: the sense that events, like history, are part of a necessary progression. In a notable section of Camus's novel, the investigating magistrate asks Meursault to recount the events surrounding his shooting of an Arab:

> He urged me to go over the day again. I went over what I'd already told him about: Raymond, the beach, the swim, the fight, the beach again, the little spring, the sun and the five shots.[7]

What is vital here, beside the matter-of-fact delivery, is the complete absence of causal relation: no 'because', no 'and so', no 'therefore'. There are no conjunctions, simply nouns and a repeated definite article. It becomes difficult to obtain any relational momentum – any material, any space, with which to construct an explanation. Also absent are any psychological insights and, particularly striking given the subject matter, any emotional content. Traditional means of narrative movement are lacking; any link here is simply a matter of chronology and not the expected causality. The cumulative effect of this is pivotal, enabling narrative to frustrate deterministic expectations and to move away from the notion of events comporting themselves around an organising necessity. For the existentialist notion of a freely choosing, non-determined self, it is imperative that events are not presented as cohering around an explanatory centre. This would be a falsification of the way in which we actually encounter the world. The world is not transparent, wholly known with an already foreseen future; it is, on the contrary, opaque, ambiguous. We cannot know the outcome of our actions and knowing, understanding, a situation is always only a retrospective activity. Søren Kierkegaard, the progenitor of philosophical existentialism, points out that life is lived forwards into an unknown, undetermined future.[8]

In his review of *The Outsider*, Sartre links Camus's style to both the philosopher David Hume and American neo-realist fiction, in particular Ernest Hemingway, noting that both make use of 'isolated impressions'. Sartre notes that in Camus's novel,

> Each sentence is a present instant, but not an indecisive one that spreads like a stain to the following one. The sentence is sharp, distinct and self-contained. It is separated by a void from the following one [. . .] The sentences in *The Outsider* are islands. We bounce from sentence to sentence, from void to void.[9]

This sense of disconnectedness illuminates our understanding of the following passage from *A Chancer*:

While one of the other team's players gathered the ball Tammas looked for the number 11 and marked him. When the throw was taken the ball was shied to the tall fellow and he tried to flick it on as he turned but Tammas was right behind him and his studs caught in the guy's sock, taking the foot from under him and he went crashing down, the ball returning out for another throw in. Tammas reached to help him up but he shook off his hand and muttered: That was fucking ridiculous.[10]

This contourless prose effects the tone of an emotionless report. The sentences are factual and describe processes, activities, with little adjectival or adverbial colour. All of the sentences carry the same narrative weight with no exclamation, no sense of a momentum and no sense of a conclusion. A football match is described with no indication of passion or any kind of emotional or intellectual involvement. As with Camus, this way of writing spreads out and infects the construction of character. Indeed, the very notion of character is rendered problematic in Kelman's texts, for the thoughts, hopes, memories, emotions, desires and so forth that traditionally constitute character are almost wholly absent. There are virtually no physical descriptions, for as I have suggested elsewhere, to describe is to *inscribe*, to render a quality essential, fixed, determined and determining.[11] Tammas, then, is less a character, more a void, an empty centre of activity. Character does not cohere, and there is a corresponding lack of community; the atomistic, shorn narrative form suggests an isolated self among other isolated selves. 'Terrible, said John, we're splitting up, we're all splitting up, we're all fucking splitting up.'[12] Here, Tammas's acquaintance John – 'friend' implies a depth of feeling and a sense of connection entirely absent – encapsulates the novel's structural and thematic ambit. There is a basic situation, 'splitting up', which is not developed or worked through, only amplified: 'We're splitting up' becomes 'we're *all* splitting up' which becomes 'we're all *fucking* splitting up.' No addition to clarity or meaning accompanies the addition of each word, simply more of the same.

Like Kelman's three previous novels, *How late it was, how late* lacks the conventions of story. Nothing much happens. There are few developments and, bar the onset of his never-explained blindness, the Sammy Samuels the reader encounters at the outset of the novel is largely the Sammy Samuels who 'disappears' at the end. Again, instead of any sense of progression, we have the typical existential statement of a basic situation. The novel begins with an allusion to Dostoevsky's *Notes from Underground* with Samuels's 'ye're no a good man, ye're just no a good man,' recalling the underground man's 'I am a sick man . . . I am an angry man.'[13] As with Dostoevsky's novel, the form and delivery of *How late* establishes a confessional immediacy. Sammy Samuels wakes in a situation and this initial narrative plunge takes us straight into the narrated situation with no contextualisation, and no guiding narrator to orient the reader. This formally mimics the existentialist notion of 'thrownness': the idea that we simply find ourselves, without explanation, within a situation. Sammy awakes and his initial thoughts move from his condition to his position: 'Where in the name of fuck . . . He was here.' The 'here' quickly assumes a malevolent quality: 'he was leaning against auld rusty palings, with pointed spikes, some missing or broke off.'[14] These palings and spikes suggest encirclement, entrapment, the bars of a prison. This notion of constraint is the thematic centre of the novel but it is more than simply a physical constraint.

> What did it matter but what did it matter; cunts looking at ye. Who gives a fuck. Just sometimes they bore their way in, some of them do anyway; they seem able to give ye a look that's more than a look: it's like when ye're a wean at school and there's this auld woman teacher who takes it serious even when you and the wee muckers are having a laugh and cracking jokes behind her back and suddenly she looks straight at ye and ye can tell she knows the score, she knows it's happening. Exactly. And it's only you. The rest dont notice. You see her and she sees you. Naybody else. Probably it's their turn next week. The now it's you she's copped. You. The jokes don't sound funny any longer. The auld bastard, she's fucked ye man. With one look. That's how easy you are. And ye see the truth then about yerself. Ye see how ye're fixed forever. Stupid wee fucking arsehole.[15]

Here, as throughout, there are a number of references to sight, to the act of looking. The novel teems with visual references and the dustjacket of the hardback edition features the symbol for a police camera, reminding us that the English word 'look' is etymologically linked to the German lugen, meaning 'to spy'. The foregrounding of scrutiny, the sense of being under permanent observation, evokes a Kafkaesque world in which the private is slowly erased as it is taken into the objective, observable world of a state bureaucracy. Both The Trial and The Castle present a world converted into a vast panopticon in which there is no possibility of a private space, a private self.[16] Kelman's novel recapitulates this, but with a subtle shift; as Sammy indicates, this look is 'more than a look'. This recollection of a classroom incident is charged with existential significance for it restates an important component of Sartrean philosophy. Samuels mentions being 'fucked' by the teacher's look and, crucially, of being 'fixed'. Sartre's model of human relations is based upon Hegel's master/slave dialectic where others are both necessary for our sense of being and simultaneously a threat to our possibilities and thus our freedom. We need to be seen in order to have a sense of our existing, but at the same time, we have no control over how we are seen. As subjects, when another looks at us we become, for them, objects, and so arises that sense of being 'fixed' to which Sammy refers. A look simultaneously conveys and denies our subjectivity. *How late* charts, then, an attempt to evade the look, to evade objectification and to resist solidification. Sammy's blindness, whether real or feigned, becomes a survival mechanism.

You Have to be Careful in the Land of the Free is, after the experiment of *Translated Accounts*, a return to more familiar Kelman territory. There are, however, some notable divergences from the style of Kelman's earlier novels. Firstly, this novel employs a first-person narrator, Jeremiah Brown, and it is Jeremiah who functions as the focaliser. Everything comes to us through Jeremiah and this enables the kind of unmediated attention to the internal that is normally absent from a Kelman text.

This method permits some temporal experimentation, for Jeremiah's narrative is suffused with moments from his past that are narrated as if still present. This chronological disturbance is a familiar modernist textual strategy intended to make time and temporality seem more personal, more lived. We are left with what Jeremiah describes as his 'ayn fantastic inner dramatics'.[17] The narrative also has a greater sense of flow; the episodic structure of the earlier novels is replaced by a more fluid, ludic form. With this, Kelman's novel becomes a kind of existentialist revision of Laurence Sterne, in particular the Sterne of *A Sentimental Education*. Sterne's playful tales move by caprice and association rather than necessity, setting themselves against the ordered controlled narratives that would indicate a rationalist Enlightenment sensibility. To rupture the lines of logical progression, Sterne famously employs elaborate digressions and apostrophes to create a circumlocutory apparatus which changes direction moment to moment to moment. Kelman's novel utilises some of these procedures but to an existential end, to achieve a kind of modified, free stream of association in which the narrative voice is untrammelled and unchecked. Jeremiah's statement that he is 'opposed to authority on principle' is mirrored by a narrative style which resists any standardised beginning-middle-end form.[18] Furthermore, Kelman follows Joyce and Sterne in the creation of neologisms and polyglot compounds as ways of unsettling standard English. For example, Jeremiah castigates 'sentimental fucking el turderro', a pseudo-Hispanic construction, and speaks of the 'parafuckingnoctic', a conglomeration of 'paranoid', the familiar Anglo-Saxon, and the hint of 'gnosis' (mystic knowledge).[19] These disorienting confections are assisted by the insertion of the oral into the written, with Americanised phonetic renderings – 'Skarrisch' – sitting beside more familiar Scotticisms such as 'mair' and 'ye'. Linguistic manipulation is a means of kicking against, resisting, formal standardised English.

Kelman uses other recognisable techniques to this end. There are the familiar Beckettian auto-cancellations, where a statement is made and then immediately retracted – 'I do not understand how that happened. Yes I do

[. . .]' – but there is a more sophisticated version of this device with its genesis in Dostoevsky.[20] This is the notion of 'patterned antinomy', the grammatical equivalent of a swinging pendulum: 'It was mair than shyness, in fact it wasnay shyness. Maybe it was extreme caution.'[21] This sentence adds to the Beckettian device above for, as well as stating and retracting, it offers a third position. In effect we have 'yes', then 'no', then 'maybe this'. Certainty is banished, infusing the narrative with the ambiguous quality that Sartre commends in the passage from *What is Literature?* quoted above.

The narrative works not by progression, but by association. Jeremiah determines where, if, it will go, but his own journey is less to do with motion than with an existential sense of groundedness.

> Part of my problem as a human being was that I didnay know how to do it properly, how to be it properly, be a human being. What the fuck do ye do? What are the appropriate actions?[22]

This quest for a way to be is apparent from the outset of the novel. The first sentence states that the narrator is 'gaun hame', but this is not a straightforwardly nationalistic tale of a homesick Scot: 'I needit to get back to something. It had nothing to do with homesickness or notions of a motherland. Fuck the motherland, blood and guts and soil and shite, it didnay matter a fuck to me.'[23] Here, Jeremiah rejects nationalism because he identifies it with fascism, with *Blud und Boden* – 'blood and soil' – an identification Kelman makes in his critical writings. Jeremiah's sense of groundlessness is not a desire for a physical return, or a nostalgic yearning for 'homecoming', but a desire for a metaphysical rootedness, a sense of connection. For Heidegger, the feeling of unhomeliness is a fundamental component of our being and leads to that most existential of moods, angst. But, Heidegger argues, it is precisely this unhomeliness that provides our freedom. The feeling of unhomeliness coupled with anxiety reveals to us that we are not fixed, not pre-cast, not determined to be anything. This leaves us anchorless, without a home, but it simultaneously entails our freedom. As readers we never quite know if Jeremiah achieves this freedom; we never know whether he arrives 'home', for the novel ends rather than closes. The suggestion may be that real freedom is only possible in artistic form, not in the extra-textual world.

Existentialist notions of freedom, then, underwrite and sustain both the form and the content of Kelman's fictions and, at first glance, a similar commitment to freedom seems to be at work in Kelman's critical prose, even a cursory reading of which reveals a strong sense of political conviction. But it is precisely these convictions that, translated into aesthetic statements, contradict the notions of freedom upon which the novels depend. As Alan Freeman points out, Kelman's characterisation of art, artists and artistic value

is 'not only peculiarly incoherent but in conflict with his artistic achievements'.[24] For Freeman, Kelman

> values art only when it has moral or political utility. From a reasonable scepti-
> cism of bourgeois elitism [Kelman] applies his own stereotype, conflating all art
> and art criticism as either revolutionary or reactionary. [. . .] The simplicities of
> 'us' and 'them' are repeated throughout Kelman's discussion of art.[25]

There are a number of useful observations here. Firstly, the notion of artistic 'utility' seems at odds with an existentialist aesthetic. Existentialism is
phenomenological; it is a *descriptive* philosophy. It does not concern itself
with how things could be, or how they ought to be, but with how they *are*.
Kelman's novels follow this prescription in that they scrupulously avoid
judging the characters or situations that they portray. That neutral quality
inherited from Camus and Robbe-Grillet brings with it a certain objectivity;
within the novels there is a sense of concrete thisness. Kelman's difficulty
is that in his critical writing he seeks to convert this kind of existential fact
into a political or moral value. That a text or an act or a language amounts
to cultural expression is a factual claim; that that act is valid or ought to be
accorded some respect is a *moral* claim. There are hard yards between fact
and value, and to save the work of constructing a bridging argument, Kelman
simply collapses the distinction. Consequently, for Kelman, a negative
reception to the work of those writers and artists he favours is always due to
some ideological contamination, never simply a question of taste or choice.
One cannot simply dislike something. You dislike it because your values are
corrupt; you have the 'wrong' set of political convictions. By insisting every
aesthetic choice is necessarily a political choice, every aesthetic judgement
necessarily a political judgement, Kelman seems at a stroke to disallow
artistic criticism. So to dislike, say, the work of Agnes Owens is equivalent
to questioning the validity of the culture of Agnes Owens. For Kelman, 'it
should go without saying that any culture, history or literature is valid.'[26]
But this approach rapidly transmutes into the problem of cultural relativism
that haunts the existentialist, the well-meaning liberal and the committed
post-structuralist. Is *Mein Kampf* valid? Is *The Protocols of the Elders of Zion*
to be taken seriously? What about homophobic or misogynistic texts? Child
pornography? Kelman cannot coherently maintain that everything is valid
and also insist that he is 'wary of folk who adopt relativist positions', for the
former is itself a form of relativism.[27]

This brings us, inevitably, to Kelman's own critical reception. If all cultures
are equally valid, if all cultural expressions are equally valid, then presumably
the notorious criticisms directed at his work from, say, Rabbi Neuberger and
Simon Jenkins are valid? Seemingly, for Kelman, they are not, for his culture

and his work are not up for evaluation 'unless he so chooses' – but this is a dispensation seemingly only available to himself.[28] Furthermore, if every discourse is valid, what if there are two mutually exclusive competing claims? This is a problem at the centre of existentialism, for if each individual is free, what happens if there are competing freedoms? When does my freedom *to* impinge upon your freedom *from*? The difficulty occurs because there is no overseeing court of appeal; hence Sartre has to introduce a kind of Kantian categorical imperative into his existentialism whereby an individual acts as if he were choosing that everyone in a similar circumstance should act in this same way. Kelman offers nothing as sophisticated as this. Instead he operates a crude check for artistic worth: either something is of the people and accords with his political principles, or it is elitist and, therefore, to be disregarded. As Douglas Dunn observes, Kelman never quite gets around to detailing precisely what is at fault in the writing of, say, Evelyn Waugh or Philip Larkin or Kingsley Amis. For Dunn, Kelman's 'differentiation of "good writer" and "bad writer" is essentially moral, and morality is to a large extent associated with the political convictions that Kelman finds obvious and necessary.'[29] In other words, what Kelman offers is a self-serving and self-vindicating tautology.

As Freeman also notes, Kelman's critical pieces are infused with a simplistic notion of 'us' and 'them', and again this seems to conflict with existentialism, as it seems to place an unexpected importance upon the communal. Consider this passage from 'The Importance of Glasgow in My Work', in which Kelman describes his initial literary impulse: 'The stories I wanted to write would derive from my own background, my own socio-cultural experience. I wanted to write as one of my own people, I wanted to write and remain a member of my own community.'[30] The weight given to 'my own people' and 'my own community' suggests a source of value beyond the personal and the individual but existentialism is absolutely, fundamentally, individualist; there can be no existential 'we'. Moreover, the very notions of 'us' and 'them' are existentially suspect, for they seem to imply that individual communities possess essential qualities that serve as markers and means of differentiation. Any ascription of essence, of underlying common properties, is, however, acutely anti-existential. Essential properties are qualities of the fixed, the final, the closed. Only the open and the possible are existential. Thus, whilst Kelman's fictions can be clearly located and accommodated within the existentialist tradition, his critical work simply cannot for it is, ultimately, clearly, essentialist.

Endnotes

Where Endnotes provide incomplete bibliographical details, a full reference will be found under 'Further Reading'.

Abbreviations
How late: *How late it was, how late*
Careful: *You Have to be Careful in the Land of the Free*

A note on newspaper sources
Section/page numbers are omitted from newspaper references, in the expectation that readers will access newspaper sources primarily via archived webpages and electronic databases (which seldom include pagination details).

Introduction – Hames

1. Alison Flood, 'James Kelman launches broadside against Scotland's literary culture', www.guardian.co.uk/books/2009/aug/27/james-kelman-scotland-literary-culture, posted 27 August 2009; accessed 27 August 2009.
2. Jasper Hamill, 'Literary Scotland torn apart over Kelman spat', *Sunday Herald* (Glasgow), 30 August 2009.
3. Kelman quoted in Flood, 'James Kelman launches broadside against Scotland's literary culture'.
4. Francis Russell Hart, *The Scottish Novel: A Critical Survey* (London: John Murray, 1978), p. ix.
5. Robert Crawford's *Scotland's Books: The Penguin History of Scottish Literature* (London: Penguin, 2007) treats J. K. Rowling as Scottish; the first Harry Potter book was written while Rowling lived in Edinburgh.
6. Kelman quoted in Flood, 'James Kelman launches broadside against Scotland's literary culture'.
7. See the Prize website, www.themanbookerprize.com/prize/man-booker-international; accessed 31 August 2009.

8. Bibliography of Scottish Literature in Translation, http://boslit.nls.uk; accessed 31 August 2009.

9. Jonathan Coe, 'Voices on the Caledonian Road', *The Guardian*, 25 April 1991.

10. Kelman insists this speech 'was not a plea for separatism, nor for nationalism, nor for the world to recognise the supremacy of Scottish culture – all of which was reported by various media'. '"And the judges said . . ."' in *"And the judges said . . ."*, p. 56. The speech itself was published as 'Elitist slurs are racism by another name' (see Further Reading for full bibliographic details).

11. Milne, 'Broken English', p. 106.

12. Attributed to Michael Schmidt in Hamill, 'Literary Scotland torn apart over Kelman spat'.

13. But see also, for example, 'Oh my darling' in *The Good Times*.

Chapter 1 – Shanks

1. See Hobsbaum, 'The Glasgow Group', pp. 58–63.

2. Kelman, 'Afterword' to *An Old Pub Near the Angel*, p. 126.

3. Kelman, '"And the judges said . . ."' in *"And the judges said . . ."*, p. 38.

4. Ibid. p. 39.

5. Ibid. pp. 39–40.

6. Kelman, 'Afterword' to *An Old Pub Near the Angel*, pp. 178–9.

7. Kelman, *An Old Pub Near the Angel*, p. 24.

8. Ibid. p. 62.

9. Ibid. p. 9.

10. Ibid. p.106. 'Nice to be Nice' also appears in *Not not while the giro* (pp. 24–32). For Kelman's brief account of the story's composition, see the 'Afterword' to *An Old Pub Near the Angel*, pp. 129–31.

11. Kelman, *An Old Pub Near the Angel*, p. 114.

12. Ibid. p.130.

13. Kelman, *Three Glasgow Writers*, p. 51.

14. Kelman, *Three Glasgow Writers*, pp. 52, 53, 55. The story was republished in *Not not while the giro* (pp. 88–100). In this version, some of the phrases that I have indicated are contracted or anglicised, so 'I mind fine' becomes simply 'I mind' (p. 89) and 'in they days' becomes 'in those days' (p. 89). Perhaps Kelman made these changes to suggest that the speaker is adopting a more formal register than might normally be the case in order to communicate his story to an unspecified third party.

15. Kelman, *Three Glasgow Writers*, p. 52.

16. Klaus, *James Kelman*, p. 3.

17. Kelman, *Not not while the giro*, p. 150. For ease of reference, all quotations from 'No Longer the Warehouseman' refer to the version of the story that appears in this collection.

18. Ibid. p. 152.
19. Regarding 'inner speech', see V. N. Volosinov, *Marxism and the Philosophy of Language*, trans. Ladislav Matejka and I. R. Titunik (London: Harvard University Press, [1929] 1973), pp. 9–17, 115–25.
20. Kelman, *Not not while the giro*, p.120. For ease of reference, the quotation from 'Jim Dandy' is taken from the version of the story that appears in this collection.
21. Kelman, *Three Glasgow Writers*, p. 69. See also *Lean Tales*, p. 36.
22. Kelman has stated that many of the stories in *Lean Tales* were taken from an abandoned novel. This might explain the sense, when reading the tales together, that they constitute fragmentary episodes from the life of a single narrator.
23. See Kelman, *Lean Tales*, pp. 12–17.
24. Kelman, *Three Glasgow Writers*, p. 71. See also *Lean Tales*, p. 38.
25. Kelman, *Some Recent Attacks*, p. 6.
26. Kelman, *Not not while the giro*, pp. 213, 204.
27. Ibid. p. 209.
28. James Kelman, unpublished interview with David Borthwick, Scott Hames and Paul Shanks, Taylor Building, University of Aberdeen, 16 May 2003.
29. Kelman, *Lean Tales*, p. 48. For ease of reference, all quotations from 'Learning the Story' refer to the version of the story that appears in this collection.
30. Ibid.
31. Ibid. p. 49.
32. 'Sarah Crosbie' is reproduced with some minor alterations in *The Burn*, pp. 123–4.
33. James Kelman, unpublished interview with David Borthwick, Scott Hames and Paul Shanks.
34. Ibid.
35. 'Getting rid of that standard third party narrative voice is getting rid of a whole value system [. . .] Let's just go for the factual reality here. [. . .] So in a sense, getting rid of the narrative voice is trying to get down to that level of pure objectivity' (McNeill, 'Interview with James Kelman', pp. 4–5).
36. Kelman, *The Busconductor Hines*, p. 101.
37. Craig, 'Resisting Arrest', pp. 107–8.
38. Kelman, *A Chancer*, p. 53.
39. Ibid.
40. The narrator of 'Lassies are trained that way' claims that 'getting paranoiac is the simplest thing in the world' (*The Burn*, pp. 160–1), and so it is for many of Kelman's protagonists.
41. Joyce, *Ulysses: The 1922 Text*, p. 7.
42. Kelman, *The Busconductor Hines*, p. 178.
43. Kelman, *A Chancer*, p. 130.
44. Kelman, *The Busconductor Hines*, p. 3.

45. Ibid. pp. 33, 21, 76.
46. Ibid. p. 128.

Chapter 2 – McGlynn

1. Julia Neuberger, 'Cooking the Booker', *Evening Standard* (London), 14 October 1994.
2. Kelman, 'Elitist slurs are racism by another name'.
3. McLean, 'James Kelman Interviewed', p. 71.
4. [no author], 'Tough icon who loves to hate the Booker', *The Sunday Times*, 11 September 1994.
5. Pierre Bourdieu, *Distinction: A Social Critique of the Judgement of Taste*, trans. Richard Nice (Cambridge, MA: Harvard University Press, 1984), p. 6.
6. Pitchford, 'How Late It Was for England', p. 696.
7. Huggan, 'Prizing "Otherness"', p. 413.
8. James English, 'Winning the Culture Game: Prizes, Awards and the Rules of Art', *New Literary History* 33.1 (Winter 2002), pp. 109–35.
9. Private correspondence with Chris Fowler of the Booker archive, 16 January 2009. She cites figures from August of 1994 compiled for Booker by Colman Getty PR.
10. Goff quoted by Caroline Lee, 'Reading public shuns writers on Booker list', *The Sunday Times*, 2 October 1994; fivefold sales claimed in [no author], 'Glaswegian gets Booker with tale of blind drunk', *The Irish Times*, 12 October 1994.
11. Pitchford, 'How Late It Was for England', p. 697.
12. Ibid.
13. See Alan Taylor, 'Prize Fight', *Scotland on Sunday*, 16 October 1994.
14. William Russell, 'Bickering Judges Give Booker to Kelman', *The Herald* (Glasgow), 12 October 1994.
15. Joan McAlpine, 'Kelman Rues Booker Prize Win', *The Sunday Times*, 4 May 2009.
16. McNeill, 'Interview with James Kelman', p. 2.
17. Martin Kirby, 'A Prufrock in Glasgow', *The New York Times*, 18 June 1989.
18. Jill Neville, 'Lessons from Glasgow: "A Disaffection"', *The Independent*, 18 February 1989.
19. McNeill, 'Interview with James Kelman', p. 2.
20. Kelman, *A Disaffection*, p. 16.
21. Adam Mars-Jones, 'In Holy Boozers', *Times Literary Supplement*, 1 April 1994; Jenkins, 'An Expletive of a Winner'.
22. Kelman, *How late*, p. 174
23. Ibid. p. 207.
24. McNeill, '"Edging Back Into Awareness"', pp. 120, 122.
25. Meek, 'Dead not Deid', p. 8.

26. McAlpine, 'Kelman Rues Booker Prize Win'.
27. McIlvanney, 'The Politics of Narrative in the Post-war Scottish Novel', p. 204.
28. Kelman, *How late*, p. 156
29. Neuberger, 'Cooking the Booker'.
30. Kelman, *How late*, p. 170
31. Klaus, 'Kelman for Beginners', pp. 128–9.
32. Kelman, *How late*, p. 222.
33. Hames, 'Eyeless in Glasgow', p. 517.
34. McIlvanney, 'The Politics of Narrative in the Post-war Scottish Novel', p. 206.
35. Kelman, *A Disaffection*, p. 85.
36. Cairns Craig, 'Scotland: Culture After Devolution', in Longley et al. (eds), *Ireland (Ulster) Scotland: Concepts, Contexts, Comparisons* (Belfast: Cló Ollscoil na Banríona, 2003), pp. 39–44, 44.
37. Kelman, *A Disaffection*, p. 160; Hames, 'Eyeless in Glasgow', p. 523.
38. Julia Llewellyn Smith, '"The Prize will be useful. I'm skint"', *The Times*, 13 October 1994.

Chapter 3 – Boxall

1. See March, *Rewriting Scotland*, p. 5.
2. Kelman, *Translated Accounts*, pp. 120–1.
3. Dickinson, 'I felt a Cleaving', *The Poems of Emily Dickinson* (Cambridge, MA: Harvard University Press, 1998), p. 379.
4. Kelman, *Translated Accounts*, p. 121.
5. Ibid.
6. Ibid. p. 120.
7. Ibid. pp. 120–1.
8. Ibid. p. 121.
9. Kelman, *Kieron Smith, boy*, p. 2.
10. Ibid. p. 5.
11. Ibid.
12. Ibid.
13. Kelman, *Careful*, p. 374.
14. Ibid. p. 389.
15. Kelman, *Kieron Smith, boy*, p. 219.
16. Ibid. p. 1.
17. Ibid.
18. Ibid.
19. Ibid. pp. 133–4.
20. Ibid. p. 41.
21. Kelman, *Translated Accounts*, p. 121.

Chapter 4 – Hunter

1. G. K. Chesterton, *Charles Dickens* (London: Methuen, 1906), p. 69.
2. Ibid.
3. Craig, 'Resisting Arrest', pp. 99–114.
4. There is a published monograph on Kelman's short stories, J. D. Macarthur's *Claiming Your Portion of Space*, but while it does indeed restrict its selection of primary material to the short stories, little attention is given to the particularities of the form or what sets it apart from the novel.
5. Elizabeth Bowen, *Collected Impressions* (London: Longmans, 1950), p. 39.
6. See McLean, 'James Kelman Interviewed', pp. 64–80; and the essays '"And the judges said . . . "' and 'Say Hello to John La Rose' in *"And the judges said . . ."*. H. Gustav Klaus reflects on Kelman's relationship to Sherwood Anderson in his essay 'Kelman for Beginners', pp. 131–2.
7. *The Collected Letters of Katherine Mansfield*, 4 vols., eds Vincent O'Sullivan and Margaret Scott (Oxford: Oxford University Press, 1984–), vol. II, p. 320.
8. McLean, 'James Kelman Interviewed', p. 79.
9. Quoted in Peter Jones (ed.), *Imagist Poetry* (Harmondsworth: Penguin, 1972), p. 129.
10. Ibid. pp. 130–1.
11. McLean, 'James Kelman Interviewed', p. 79.
12. *Lean Tales*, pp. 48–9. For ease of reference, all quotations from 'Learning the Story' refer to the version of the story that appears in this collection.
13. Craig, 'Resisting Arrest', p. 101.
14. Kelman, *Not not while the giro*, p. 121.
15. Ibid. p. 4.
16. Klaus, *James Kelman*, p. 6.
17. Kirk, 'Figuring the Dispossessed', p. 110.
18. Kelman, *"And the judges said . . ."*, p. 302.
19. Maley, 'Denizens, citizens, tourists', p. 66.
20. Lukács, *Writer and Critic*, p. 144.
21. Lukács, *Meaning of Contemporary Realism*, p. 35.
22. Kelman, *Greyhound for Breakfast*, p. 14.
23. Ibid. p. 8.
24. Ibid. p. 13.
25. Kelman, *The Burn*, p. 7.
26. Kelman, *The Good Times*, p. 69.
27. Ibid. p. 169.
28. Ibid. p. 174.
29. Ibid. p. 172.
30. Ibid. p. 175.
31. Kelman, *Not not while the giro*, p. 206.

32. Ibid. p. 203.
33. Ibid. p. 213.
34. Douglas Gifford, 'Discovering Lost Voices', *Books in Scotland* 38 (1991), pp. 1–6, 3–4.
35. *"And the judges said . . ."*, p. 273.
36. McNeill, 'Interview with James Kelman', p. 9.

Chapter 5 – Carter

1. Kelman, *A Disaffection*, p. 320.
2. Johnson, *Mi Revalueshanary Fren* (Keene, NY: Ausable, 2002), p. 9.
3. Kelman, 'Elitist slurs are racism by another name'.
4. Personal correspondence with James Kelman, 2 February 2009.
5. Simon Kövesi mistakenly recirculates the story that Kelman 'attempted to deliver his winner's speech, and was cut off after thirty seconds' at the Booker award ceremony (*James Kelman*, p. 159). Several newspaper articles also present the event in this way (see *Scotland on Sunday*, 'Supplement', 16 October 1994; *The Sunday Times*, 'The Speech he had no time to make at the Booker ceremony', 16 October 1994). Kelman reports that only the BBC television *broadcast* was cut off when the network returned to the studio for the critics' commentary. He attributes the cut-off to 'media inefficiency' rather than malice or censorship. The cessation of the broadcast happened to precede the speech and coincide with Kelman's collection of the cheque from the Award committee's Chairperson (personal correspondence with James Kelman, 2 February 2009).
6. Black, 'Kelman lines up his next shot'. See (in chronological order): Daly, 'Your Average Working Kelman'; Freeman, 'The Humanist's Dilemma'; Crumey, '"And the Judges Said . . ."'; Eagleton, 'James Kelman'; Goring, 'Smashing the state of creative writing'.
7. Goring, 'Smashing the state of creative writing', p. 16. In common with several other interviewers, Goring makes a point of noting how gently spoken and gentlemanly Kelman is in person.
8. Kelman, '"And the judges said . . ."' in *"And the judges said . . ."*, p. 68. Kelman's discomfort with institutions in general is articulated in a number of essays and interviews; see his discussions of party politics in 'K is for culture' and Vericat, 'An Interview with James Kelman'.
9. Kelman, 'Afterword' to *An Old Pub Near the Angel*, p. 182.
10. Ibid.
11. To be fair, Kelman admits to going off on 'rants' and experiencing 'bouts of irritated frustration' ('Introduction' to *"And the judges said . . ."*, pp. 4, 20). My point is that the monovocality of the essays tends to reinforce Kelman's stereotypical depiction, enabling the too-easy dismissal of his political writing's substance.

12. David Robinson, 'Plain-talking Glaswegian', *The Scotsman*, 26 April 2008.
13. Kelman, *A Disaffection*, pp. 320–1.
14. Eagleton, 'James Kelman', pp. 263–4.
15. Freeman, 'The Humanist's Dilemma', pp. 28, 34.
16. McAlpine, 'How the Booker bust James Kelman'.
17. Freeman, 'The Humanist's Dilemma', p. 31.
18. Ibid. p. 40.
19. Ibid. pp. 32, 34.
20. Ibid. p. 34.
21. Kelman, 'Afterword' to *An Old Pub Near the Angel*, p. 182.
22. Kelman, 'A Look at Franz Kafka's Three Novels', in "*And the judges said . . .*", pp. 275, 282.
23. Ibid. pp. 299, 311.
24. Ibid. p. 334. Bill Dodds notes that 'Kafka was certainly familiar with, and appears to have been sympathetic to, radical political theory of the left, but neither his biography nor his fiction suggests that he subscribed to a conventional political philosophy or programme, with the possible exception of ethical anarchism.' 'The case for a political reading' in Julian Preece (ed.), *The Cambridge Companion to Kafka* (London: Cambridge University Press, 2002), pp. 131–50, 146–7.
25. See Walter Benjamin, 'G: Exhibitions, Advertising, Grandvilles', in *The Arcades Project*, trans. Howard Eiland and Kevin McLaughlin (Cambridge, MA: Belknap, Harvard University, 1999), pp. 180–97.
26. Walter Benjamin, *Illuminations*, ed. Hannah Arendt, trans. Harry Zohn (New York: Schocken, 1968), p. 257.
27. Kelman, 'A Reading from the Work of Noam Chomsky and the Scottish Tradition in the Philosophy of Common Sense' in "*And the judges said . . .*", pp. 164, 174–5.
28. Ibid. pp. 140–86.
29. Kövesi, *James Kelman*, p. 4.
30. The 'Introduction' to "*And the judges said . . .*" provides a comprehensive view of Kelman's activist campaigns and experiences.
31. Fanon, 'On National Culture', in *The Wretched of the Earth*, trans. Constance Farrington (New York: Grove, 1963), pp. 206–48, p. 220.
32. Ibid. pp. 222–3.
33. Ibid. pp. 220–3.
34. Kelman, 'An Interview with John La Rose' in "*And the judges said . . .*", p. 230.
35. Ibid. p. 232.
36. McAlpine, 'How the Booker bust James Kelman'.
37. Ibid.
38. Ibid.
39. Kelman, "*And the judges said . . .*", pp. 187–93.

40. Kelman, *Some Recent Attacks*, pp. 85–91.
41. Kelman, 'Afterword' to *An Old Pub Near the Angel*, p. 139.
42. Kelman, 'An Interview with John La Rose' in *"And the judges said . . ."*, p. 243.
43. Kelman, 'Shouting at the Edinburgh Fringe Forum' in *"And the judges said . . ."*, p. 79.
44. Kelman, 'ATTACK NOT RACIST, say police' in *"And the judges said . . ."*, p. 112.
45. Ibid. p. 103.
46. Ibid. pp. 106–7.
47. Ibid. p. 106.
48. Ibid. pp. 103–4.
49. Barnes, 'Down and out in Glesga low life'.
50. See for example, Kelman's discussion of postcolonial studies and 'The American School' in Tom Toremans's interview with Kelman and Alasdair Gray; of creative writing programmes in an interview with Rosemary Goring ('Smashing the State of Creative Writing'); and the 'Afterword' to *An Old Pub Near the Angel*.
51. Kelman, 'Introduction' to *"And the judges said . . ."*, p. 11.
52. McAlpine, 'How the Booker bust James Kelman'.
53. The introductions to *Some Recent Attacks* and *"And the judges said . . ."* document the very broad range of causes to which the author has long been committed. Kelman has also been the champion of censored, exiled, imprisoned and murdered writers, including Taslima Nasrin (Bangladesh), Ken Saro-Wiwa (Nigeria), and the Kurdish writer, Ismail Besikci, to name a few.
54. Kelman, 'Foreword' to *Some Recent Attacks*, p. 4.
55. Kelman, '"And the judges said . . ."' in *"And the judges said . . ."*, p. 42. Leonard's poem can be found in the collection *Situations Theoretical and Contemporary* (Newcastle: Galloping Dog, 1996).
56. Kelman, 'Afterword' to *An Old Pub Near the Angel*, p. 152.
57. Klaus, *James Kelman*, pp. 53–5.
58. Kelman, 'Introduction' to *"And the judges said . . ."*, p. 16.
59. Kelman, 'Artists and Value' in *Some Recent Attacks*, p. 9.
60. Kelman's twelve-year-old memories of being a newspaper boy, and confession about intentionally ditching his younger brothers, strongly recall Kieron and his emotionally distant older brother, Matt. Kelman, 'When I Was That Age Did Art Exist?' in *"And the judges said . . ."*, p. 418.
61. Kelman, 'When I Was That Age Did Art Exist?' in *"And the judges said . . ."*, p. 425.
62. An early version of the essay took six months to write ('Introduction' to *"And the judges said . . ."*, p. 14) and can be found in *Edinburgh Review* 84 (1990) as 'A Reading from Noam Chomsky and the Scottish Tradition in

the Philosophy on Common Sense'. The essay is also included in *"And the judges said . . ."*, pp. 140–87.

63. See Kelman's 'Afterword' to *An Old Pub Near the Angel*, extracts of which appeared as 'Make yer point' in *The Guardian* (11 August 2007), and 'James Kelman's LA Story' in *Scotland on Sunday Review* (12 August 2007).

64. In the interest of full disclosure: James Kelman is a personal friend and has been a cherished colleague at the University of Texas at Austin. I have shared the history of my relationship with Kelman with the editor and publisher. I am also the Mia Carter to whom the essay, 'When I Was That Age Did Art Exist?' in *"And the judges said. . ."* is dedicated. I am not sure that I have ever believed in total or complete objectivity; all I can say is that this chapter is written with scholarly integrity and intellectual and emotional openness. My thanks to the editor for so generously sharing with me many resources that would have been challenging to locate here in the United States.

Chapter 6 – Archibald

1. Quoted in Anderson, 'The War Against Silence: An Interview with James Kelman'.

2. I am grateful to James Kelman for supplying me with up-to-date versions of his work and the accompanying text 'Quick notes on twelve plays'. These notes read as if they are addressed to someone interested in staging Kelman's work in the US, presumably Rude Mechanicals: www.rudemechs.com.

3. All years refer to the date of the first production of each play. *The Busker* is a development of the short story 'Old Holborn', published in the collection *Lean Tales*.

4. *They Make These Noises* is a development of the short story 'Circumstances' (published in *An Old Pub Near the Angel*), which was later reworked as 'Ten Guitars' in *Not not while the giro*.

5. *Man to Man* also appeared in a collection of work by Glasgow artist, Stuart Murray, entitled *In Pubs* (Glasgow: Streetlevel Gallery, 2007).

6. The short story 'Comic Cuts' (published in the collection *The Good Times*) was the basis for both *The Art of the Big Bass Drum* and *The Soup Enigma*.

7. According to Kelman, the Scottish actor Jim Twaddale performed a stage version of *In With the Doctor* as a monologue in the Netherbow Arts Centre, Edinburgh, in the early 1980s. Private correspondence, 2 June 2009.

8. *Unlucky* and *The Hitchhiker* are screen versions of short stories of the same name, published, respectively, in *The Burn* and *Not not while the giro*. The short story on which *A Situation* is based also appears in *The Burn*.

9. Private correspondence with Kelman, 2 February 2009.

10. See news item at www.scottishscreen.com/news/news_story_quick.php?news_id=698. Glenaan has performed in Kelman plays on both radio and stage.

11. The eleven adaptations or developments of previous work are *A Situation/ The Spanner in the Works*, *They Make These Noises*, *The Soup Enigma*, *How late it was, how late*, *In With the Doctor*, *He Knew Him Well*, *The Busconductor Hines*, *Unlucky*, *The Busker*, *The Hitchhiker* and *Man to Man*.
12. Kövesi, *James Kelman*, p. 30.
13. The pair were sentenced under English-influenced Scots law, hanged and beheaded. See P. Berresford Ellis and Seumas Mac a' Ghobhainn, *The Scottish Insurrection of 1820* (Edinburgh: John Donald, [1970] 2001).
14. Kelman, *Hardie and Baird & Other Plays*, p. 109; Kelman, 'Quick notes on twelve plays'.
15. II, i (*Hardie and Baird & Other Plays*, p. 163).
16. II, v (Ibid. p. 173).
17. II, vi (Ibid. p. 180).
18. Act II (Ibid. p.100).
19. See Francis Fukuyama, *The End of History and the Last Man* (Penguin: London, 1993).
20. Workers' City was a campaign criticising the official celebration of Glasgow as 1990 European City of Culture. The name, Kelman writes, 'was chosen to directly challenge "Merchant City"' and the sanitised, pro-capitalist image of Glasgow culture and history local officials wished to promote. See Kelman's 'Foreword' to *Some Recent Attacks*, and pp. 44–56 of '"And the judges said ..."' in *"And the judges said ..."*.
21. Kövesi, *James Kelman*, p. 7.
22. Kelman, 'Quick notes on twelve plays'.
23. Kelman, *Hardie and Baird & Other Plays*, p. 8.
24. Kelman, 'Quick notes on twelve plays'.
25. Klaus, *James Kelman*, p. 77.
26. McNeill, 'Interview with James Kelman', p. 9.
27. For a contemporary account of the executions see www.nls.uk/broadsides/broadside.cfm/id/14670/criteria/stirling (accessed 30 August 2009).
28. I, vii (*Hardie and Baird & Other Plays*, p. 135).
29. Of course, the plays of Samuel Beckett remain the most famous example of a writer 'directing' a play's characters.
30. Ian Black, 'Kelman lines up his next shot', *The Sunday Times*, 16 October 1994. The play Kelman refers to is *One, Two – Hey!*
31. Kelman, *Hardie and Baird & Other Plays*, p. 107.
32. The cast of *One, Two – Hey!*, which was produced on a profit-share basis, numbered thirteen and included a seven-piece band.
33. Clark, 'A conversation with James Kelman'.
34. Kövesi, *James Kelman*, p. 4.
35. Ibid. pp. 2–3.
36. Joyce McMillan, 'Herbal Remedies / Blood Brothers', *The Scotsman*, 19 October 2007.

37. Mark Brown, 'Herbal Remedies / Antigone: Park-bench philosophy hits new heights', *Daily Telegraph*, 23 October 2007.
38. Mark Fisher, 'Herbal Remedies', *The Guardian*, 19 October 2007.
39. David Pollock, 'Herbal Remedies', *Financial Times*, 27 October 2007.
40. McMillan, 'Herbal Remedies / Blood Brothers'.

Chapter 7 – Craig

1. Kelman, *Three Glasgow Writers*, p. 51.
2. Kelman, '"And the judges said . . ."' in *"And the judges said . . ."*, p. 41.
3. Kelman, *How late*, p. 374.
4. Alasdair Gray, *Lanark: A Life in Four Books* (Edinburgh: Canongate, [1981] 2007), p. 122.
5. Kelman, *The Busconductor Hines*, p. 88.
6. Kelman, '"And the judges said . . ."' in *"And the judges said . . ."*, p. 41.
7. Kelman, 'Elitism and English Literature, Speaking as a Writer' in *"And the judges said . . ."*, pp. 64–5.
8. See 'Afterword' to *An Old Pub Near the Angel*, p. 130. 'If I had [known Leonard's poetry], it would have affected my work, and that particular story ['Nice to be Nice'] would have been altered fundamentally.' The entirety of *Six Glasgow Poems* is reprinted in Leonard's collection *Intimate Voices*, and also appears on his website: www.tomleonard.co.uk.
9. See cover of Leonard, *Intimate Voices*.
10. Kelman, 'Afterword' to *An Old Pub Near the Angel*, p. 152.
11. Ibid. pp. 182, 183.
12. Kelman, '"And the judges said . . ."' in *"And the judges said . . ."*, p. 41.
13. Chomsky, *Problems of Knowledge and Freedom*, p. 26.
14. Kelman, 'A Reading from the Work of Noam Chomsky' in *"And the judges said . . ."*, p. 156.
15. Chomsky quoted by Kelman, Ibid.
16. Ibid.
17. Ibid. p. 185.
18. Chomsky, *Problems of Knowledge and Freedom*, p. 46.
19. Kelman, 'A Reading from the Work of Noam Chomsky' in *"And the judges said . . ."*, pp. 184, 186.
20. Kelman, 'Afterword' to *An Old Pub Near the Angel*, p. 182.
21. Kelman, '"And the judges said . . ."' in *"And the judges said . . ."*, p. 41.
22. Kelman, *A Chancer*, pp. 135–6.
23. See John Corbett, *Language and Scottish Literature*, pp. 128–51.
24. Kelman, *A Chancer*, p. 377.
25. Kelman, *The Busconductor Hines*, p. 195.
26. Ibid.
27. Ibid., pp. 152–3.

28. Kelman, *A Disaffection*, p. 67.
29. Ibid. p. 226.
30. Ibid. p. 252.
31. Ibid. p. 313.
32. See Jameson, *The Prison-House of Language*.
33. Kelman, *A Disaffection*, p. 209.
34. Chomsky, *Problems of Knowledge and Freedom*, pp. 165, 195.
35. Kelman, *How late*, p. 1.
36. For an extended discussion of looking, seeing and Western art see Peter Brooks, *Realist Vision* (London: Yale University Press, 2005).
37. Kelman, *How late*, pp. 271–2.
38. Ibid. p. 91.
39. Ibid. p. 172.
40. Ibid. p. 255.

Chapter 8 – Hames

1. Alan Clark, 'A Prize Insult to the Courage of Scotland's Finest', *The Mail on Sunday*, 23 October 1994.
2. Kelman, 'Afterword' to *An Old Pub Near the Angel*, p. 124.
3. Meek, 'Dead not Deid', p. 8.
4. Kelman, 'Elitism and English Literature' in *"And the judges said . . ."*, p. 64.
5. *Oxford English Dictionary* ('vernacular'), dictionary.oed.com.
6. Colin MacCabe, *James Joyce and the Revolution of the Word*, p. 15.
7. Kelman, 'Afterword' to *An Old Pub Near the Angel*, p. 136.
8. See Jacques Derrida, *Of Grammatology*, trans. Gayatri Chakravorty Spivak (Baltimore, MD: Johns Hopkins University Press, 1974).
9. Tom Paulin, *The Faber Book of Vernacular Verse* (London: Faber, 1990), p. x.
10. Derek Attridge, *Joyce Effects* (Cambridge: Cambridge University Press, 2000), p. 72. For a study of this paradox in earlier Scottish writing, see Penny Fielding, *Writing and Orality*.
11. Kelman, 'Afterword' to *An Old Pub Near the Angel*, p. 127.
12. Ibid. p. 130.
13. Kelman, *Careful*, p. 215.
14. Kelman, *How late*, p. 334.
15. Ashcroft, *Caliban's Voice*, p. 3.
16. Ibid. p. 4.
17. Kelman, *How late*, p. 11.
18. Derek Attridge, *Peculiar Language: Literature as Difference from the Renaissance to Joyce* (London: Methuen, 1988), p. 57.
19. See Spinks, '"In Juxtaposition to Which?"'
20. Attridge, *Peculiar Language*, p. 54.

21. See Kelman, 'Elitism and English Literature, Speaking as a Writer' in *"And the judges said . . ."*, pp. 57–74, 64–5.
22. Shklovsky, *Theory of Prose*, p. 2.
23. Jameson, *The Prison-House of Language*, p. 51.
24. Shklovsky, *Theory of Prose*, pp. 5–6. The coinage 'enstrangement' is preferred to 'estrangement' by Shklovsky's translator because it highlights the active, positive and imaginative character of this process. See *Theory of Prose*, pp. xviii–xix.
25. Ibid. p. 12.
26. Jameson, *The Prison-House of Language*, pp. 49–50.
27. Shklovsky, *Theory of Prose*, p. 12.
28. Ibid. pp. 12–13.
29. William Wordsworth, *Preface* to *Lyrical Balads* [1802 edition], extracts in Duncan Wu, (ed.), *Romanticism: An Anthology*, 2nd edn (Oxford: Blackwell, 1998), pp. 357–63, 357.
30. Attridge, *Peculiar Language*, pp. 61–2.
31. Kelman, *A Disaffection*, p. 1.
32. Ibid.
33. Ibid. p. 10.
34. Ibid. p. 2.
35. Ibid. p. 10.
36. Ibid. p. 9.
37. Ibid. pp. 82–3.
38. Ibid. p. 5.
39. Ibid. p. 9.
40. Ibid. p. 222.
41. Ibid. p. 163.
42. Kelman, 'Artists and Value' in *Some Recent Attacks*, p. 12.
43. Kelman, *A Disaffection*, p. 211.
44. James Rolleston, *Kafka's Narrative Theatre* (London: Penn State University Press, 1974), p. 132.
45. Kafka, *The Complete Stories*, pp. 360–1. 'Josephine the Singer, or the Mouse Folk' trans. Willa and Edwin Muir.
46. Ibid. p. 367.
47. Ibid. pp. 372, 374.
48. Ibid. pp. 362, 368.
49. Kelman, *A Disaffection*, p. 10.
50. Kelman, 'I was asking a question too' in *The Good Times*, pp. 61–2.

Chapter 9 – Gardiner

1. Casanova, *The World Republic of Letters*, p. 282.
2. Ibid. p. 294.

3. See Aaron Kelly, 'James Kelman and the Deterritorialisation of Power'.
4. See Franco Moretti, 'Conjectures on World Literature', in *Debating World Literature*, ed. Christopher Prendergast (London: Verso, 2004), pp. 148–62, and Fredric Jameson, 'In the Mirror of Alternate Modernities', in Karatani Kojin, *The Origins of Modern Japanese Literature* (Durham, NC: Duke University Press, 1993), pp. vii–xx.
5. Casanova, *The World Republic of Letters*, p. 250.
6. Jenkins, 'An Expletive of a Winner'.
7. See Sarah Brouillard, *Postcolonial Writers in the Global Literary Marketplace* (Basingstoke: Palgrave, 2007).
8. Nicholas Wroe, 'Glasgow Kith', *The Guardian*, 2 June 2001.
9. Talib, *The Language of Postcolonial Literatures*, p. 22.
10. Pitchford, 'How Late It Was For England', p. 702. Italics in original. Cf. McGlynn, '"Middle-Class Wankers" and Working-Class Texts', p. 3.
11. Ashcroft et al., *The Empire Writes Back*, p. 54.
12. Craig, *Out of History*, p. 21.
13. Salman Rushdie, *Imaginary Homelands: Essays and Criticisms 1981–1991*, 2nd edn (London: Granta, 1992), pp. 9–21.
14. Boehmer, *Colonial and Postcolonial Literature*, p. 206.
15. Kelman, 'The Comfort' in *The Good Times*, pp. 194–5.
16. Talib, *The Language of Postcolonial Literatures*, pp. 90–9.
17. Selvon, *The Lonely Londoners*, pp. 87–8.
18. Deleuze and Guattari, *Kafka: Toward a Minor Literature*, pp. 28, 41.
19. Milne, 'Broken English', p. 110.
20. See Kelman, *How late*, pp. 238, 300.
21. See Kelman, *How late*, pp. 10, 12 and Michael Gardiner, 'Endless Enlightenment: Eye-Operated Technology and the Political Economy of Vision', *Reconstruction* 4.1 (2004), http://reconstruction.eserver.org.
22. Baker, '"Wee Stories With a Working-Class Theme"', p. 243.
23. See Hagemann, 'Postcolonial Translation Studies and James Kelman's *Translated Accounts*'.
24. Kelman, 'Amos Tutuola: Weaver of Fantasy'.
25. Ashcroft et al., *The Empire Writes Back*, p. 66.
26. Tutuola, *The Palm-Wine Drinkard*, p. 9.
27. See Iain Lambert, 'The Language of James Kelman, Amos Tutuola, and Ken Saro-Wiwa', in Michael Gardiner et al. (eds), *Scottish Literature and Postcolonial Literature* (Edinburgh: Edinburgh University Press, forthcoming).
28. Ashcroft et al., *The Empire Writes Back*, p. 67.
29. Kelman, 'Amos Tutuola: Weaver of Fantasy'.
30. Saro-Wiwa, *Sozaboy*, pp. 11, 15, 75.
31. Ibid. pp. 46–7.
32. Rushdie, *Imaginary Homelands*, pp. 9–21; cf. George Lamming, *The Pleasures of Exile* (Ann Arbor, MI: University of Michigan Press, 1992).

33. Kelman, *Careful*, pp. 159, 178.
34. Alasdair Gray, *Lanark: A Life in Four Books* (Edinburgh: Canongate, [1981] 2007), p. 497.
35. Kelman, *Translated Accounts*, p. 292; Kelman, *Careful*, pp. 230, 233.
36. See Ken Saro-Wiwa, *A Month and a Day: A Detention Diary* (London: Penguin, 1995), p. 33, and William Boyd's introduction to the same text, pp. x–xi. On North Sea oil see Chris Harvie, *Fool's Gold: The Story of North Sea Oil* (London: Hamish Hamilton, 1994).
37. Chinua Achebe et al., 'The Case of Ken Saro-Wiwa', *New York Review of Books* 42.7 (1995), www.nybooks.com/articles/1913.
38. Saro-Wiwa, 'Trial Speech of Ken Saro-Wiwa', http://en.wikisource.org/wiki/Trial_Speech_of_Ken_Saro-Wiwa.
39. Ken Saro-Wiwa, *Prisoners of Jebs* (Port Harcourt: Saros International, 1988), p. 10. See also Solomon Odiri Ejeke, 'The Socio-Political Dimensions of Ken Saro-Wiwa's Activism' in *Before I Am Hanged: Ken Saro-Wiwa, Literature, Politics, and Dissent*, ed. Onookome Okome (Trenton, NJ: Africa World Press, 2000).
40. Kelman, *Translated Accounts*, p. 163.
41. Ibid. p. 102.
42. Chinua Achebe, 'English and the African Writer', *Transition* 18 (1965), pp. 27–30.
43. Kelman, *Translated Accounts*, pp. 87–8.
44. Ibid. p. 244.
45. Kelman, *Careful*, p. 253.
46. See Suzanne Césaire, '1943: Le Surréalisme et Nous', *Tropiques* 8–9 (1943), pp. 14–18, and Aimé Césaire, *Notebook of a Return to the Native Land*, trans. Clayton Eshleman (Middletown, CT: Wesleyan University Press, [1939] 1995).
47. Brathwaite, *History of the Voice*, p. 55.
48. See Fredric Jameson, 'In the Mirror of Alternate Modernities', in Karatani Kojin, *The Origins of Modern Japanese Literature* (Durham, NC: Duke University Press, 1993), pp. vii–xx, and Craig, *Out of History*.

Chapter 10 – Jones

1. Kelman, *How late*, p. 172.
2. McMillan, 'Wilting, or the "Poor Wee Boy Syndrome"', p. 41.
3. Whyte, 'Masculinities in Contemporary Scottish Fiction', p. 275.
4. Kelman, 'Afterword' to *An Old Pub Near the Angel*, p. 182.
5. Jenkins, 'An Expletive of a Winner'.
6. Kelman, *How late*, p. 172.
7. R. W. Connell, *Masculinities*, 2nd edn (Berkeley and Los Angeles: University of California Press, [1995] 2005), p. 164.

8. Kelman, *How late*, p. 175.
9. McNeill, 'Interview with James Kelman', p. 4.
10. Kelman, 'Elitist slurs are racism by another name'.
11. Sally Robinson makes this argument in her analysis of representations of men in North American texts since the 1960s. She perceives a noticeable trend in the number of portrayals of white men as visibly wounded victims and argues that these representations take part in a process of recentralising white men through victimhood, 'perform[ing] the cultural work of recentering white masculinity by decentering it'. *Marked Men: White Masculinity in Crisis* (New York: Columbia University Press, 2000), p. 12.
12. Knights, *Writing Masculinities*, p. 192.
13. McMillan, 'Wilting, or the "Poor Wee Boy Syndrome"', p. 41.
14. Hegemonic masculinity is defined by Connell in his influential study *Masculinities* as 'the configuration of gender practice which embodies the currently accepted answer to the problem of the legitimacy of patriarchy, which guarantees (or is taken to guarantee) the dominant position of men and the subordination of women' (*Masculinities*, p. 77). Such a configuration defines the normative in any particular period, and can encompass, for example, the privileging of heterosexuality, fatherhood, success in work and play, and, in Western terms, whiteness, the middle class and the middle-aged.
15. Kelman, *Careful*, pp. 37, 173.
16. Kelman, *A Disaffection*, p. 1.
17. Kelman, *How late*, p. 1.
18. Kelman, *Careful*, p. 20.
19. Kelman, *How late*, p. 172.
20. Hysteria, derived from the Greek word for 'uterus', was traditionally associated with women signalling their irrational nature compared with male rationality: 'The idea of hysteria orbits around a loss of control consequent upon the invasion of the "rational" by the somatic, specifically by the womb and its folklores' (Knights, *Writing Masculinities*, p. 190).
21. Hames, 'Dogged Masculinities', p. 85.
22. Jane Gallop, *Thinking Through the Body* (New York: Columbia University Press, 1988), p. 7.
23. Margrit Shildrick, *Leaky Bodies and Boundaries: Feminism, Postmodernism and (Bio)ethics* (London: Routledge, 1997), pp. 34–5.
24. Hames, 'Dogged Masculinities', pp. 68, 69. See also Peter Middleton's *The Inward Gaze: Masculinity and Subjectivity in Modern Culture* (London: Routledge, 1992).
25. Hames, 'Dogged Masculinities', p. 69.
26. Kelman, *How late*, p. 175.
27. Kelman, *The Busconductor Hines*, p. 191.
28. Kelman, *How late*, p. 262.

29. Kelman, *A Disaffection*, p. 1.
30. Kelman, *Careful*, p. 211.
31. Kelman, *The Good Times*, p. 231.
32. Kelman, *The Busconductor Hines*, pp. 150–1.
33. See particularly McMillan, 'Wilting, or the "Poor Wee Boy Syndrome"'.
34. Ibid. pp. 48, 49.
35. See also 'Oh my darling' in *The Good Times*, pp. 68–84.
36. Kelman, *A Disaffection*, pp. 314–15.
37. Ibid. p. 315.
38. Kelman, *How late*, p. 139.
39. Kelman, *Careful*, p. 73.
40. Kövesi, *James Kelman*, p. 97.
41. Kelman, *How late*, p. 111.
42. Ibid. p. 101.
43. Ibid. p. 111.
44. Ibid. p. 101.
45. Ibid. p. 12.
46. Ibid. p. 374.
47. Kelman, *A Disaffection*, p. 337.
48. Kelman, *Kieron Smith, boy*, p. 422.
49. Steve McQueen: *How late*, p. 139; Gary Cooper: *The Good Times*, p. 83.
50. Calvin Thomas, *Male Matters: Masculinity, Anxiety and the Male Body on the Line* (Urbana and Chicago: University of Illinois Press, 1996), p. 30.
51. Judith Butler, 'Force of Fantasy', *Differences: A Journal of Feminist Cultural Studies* 2.2 (1990), pp. 105–25, 124.

Chapter 11 – Nicoll

1. Walter Kaufmann, *Existentialism from Dostoevsky to Sartre* (Cleveland, OH: Meridian, 1970), p. 12.
2. Anne Stevenson, 'Off the Buses' [1973], reprinted in Kelman, *An Old Pub Near the Angel*, pp. 117–20.
3. Kelman, 'And the judges said . . .' in *"And the judges said . . ."*, pp. 38–56, 38–9.
4. Milan Kundera, *The Art of the Novel*, trans. Linda Asher (London: Faber & Faber, 1988), p. 5. See also Kundera's *The Curtain*, trans. Linda Asher (London: Faber & Faber, 2007).
5. Sartre, *What is Literature?*, p. 166.
6. Although published after *The Busconductor Hines*, *A Chancer* is the earlier novel.
7. Camus, *The Outsider*, p. 66.
8. 'It is quite true what philosophy says: that life must be understood backwards. But then one forgets the other principle: that it must be lived forwards.'

Søren Kierkegaard, *Papers and Journals: A Selection*, ed. and trans. Alastair Hannay (Harmondsworth: Penguin, 1996), p. 161.

9. Jean-Paul Sartre, 'Camus' "The Outsider"', *Literary Essays*, trans. Annette Michelson (New York: Philosophical Library, 1957), pp. 24–41, 37, 38.

10. Kelman, *A Chancer*, p. 116.

11. Nicoll, 'Facticity, or Something Like That', p. 65.

12. Kelman, *A Chancer*, p. 173.

13. Kelman, *How late*, p. 1; Dostoevsky, *Notes from Underground*, p. 15.

14. Kelman, *How late*, p. 1.

15. Ibid. p. 12.

16. On the 'panopticon' model of control-by-surveillance, see Michel Foucault, *Discipline and Punish*, trans. Alan Sheridan (London: Penguin, [1975] 1991), pp. 195–231.

17. Kelman, *Careful*, p. 276.

18. Ibid. p. 12.

19. Ibid. pp. 71, 37.

20. Ibid. p. 21.

21. Ibid. p. 76. I borrow the term from W. Woodin Rowe's 'Dosteovskian Patterned Antinomy and its Function in *Crime and Punishment*', *Slavic and East European Journal*, 16.3 (Autumn 1972), pp. 287–96.

22. Kelman, *Careful*, pp. 120–1.

23. Ibid. pp. 26–7.

24. Freeman, 'The Humanist's Dilemma', p. 28.

25. Ibid. p. 31.

26. Kelman, 'Oppression and Solidarity' in *Some Recent Attacks*, p. 71.

27. Kelman, '"And the judges said . . ."' in *"And the judges said . . ."*, p. 52.

28. Ibid. p. 40.

29. Dunn, 'I'm right, and good, you're bad', p. 5.

30. Kelman, 'The Importance of Glasgow in My Work' in *Some Recent Attacks*, p. 81.

Further Reading

Works by James Kelman

Novels

Kelman, James, *The Busconductor Hines* (Edinburgh: Polygon/Birlinn, [1984] 2007)

Kelman, James, *A Chancer* (Edinburgh: Polygon/Birlinn, [1985] 2007)

Kelman, James, *A Disaffection* (London: Vintage, [1989] 1999)

Kelman, James, *How late it was, how late* (London: Vintage, [1994] 1998)

Kelman, James, *Translated Accounts* (Edinburgh: Polygon/Birlinn, [2001] 2009)

Kelman, James, *You Have to be Careful in the Land of the Free* (London: Hamish Hamilton, 2004)

Kelman, James, *Kieron Smith, boy* (London: Hamish Hamilton, 2008)

Collections of Short Stories

Kelman, James, *An Old Pub Near the Angel and Other Stories* (Edinburgh: Polygon/Birlinn, [1973] 2007)

Kelman, James (with Alex Hamilton and Tom Leonard), *Three Glasgow Writers* (Glasgow: Molendinar, 1976)

Kelman, Jim, *Short Tales from the Night Shift* (Glasgow: Glasgow Print Studio, 1978)

Kelman, James, *Not not while the giro* (Edinburgh: Polygon/Birlinn, [1983] 2007)

Kelman, James (with Agnes Owens and Alasdair Gray), *Lean Tales* (London: Vintage, [1985] 1995)

Kelman, James, *Greyhound for Breakfast* (Edinburgh: Polygon/Birlinn, [1987] 2008)

Kelman, James, *The Burn* (Edinburgh: Polygon/Birlinn, [1991] 2009)

Kelman, James, *The Good Times* (Edinburgh: Polygon/Birlinn [1998] 2009)

Kelman, James, *If it is your life* (London: Hamish Hamilton, 2010)

Essays, Plays and Other

Kelman, James, *Hardie and Baird & Other Plays* (London: Secker & Warburg, 1991)

Kelman, James, *Some Recent Attacks: Essays Cultural and Political* (Stirling: AK, 1992)

Kelman, James, 'Elitist slurs are racism by another name', *Scotland on Sunday*, 16 October 1994. [Booker Prize acceptance speech]

Kelman, James, 'Amos Tutuola: Weaver of Fantasy', *The Guardian*, 16 June 1997. [Obituary]

Kelman, James, 'Human Writes', *Scottish Trade Union Review* 89 (July–August 1998), pp. 32–4. [Report on human rights abuses in Turkey]

Kelman, James, "And the judges said . . .": *Essays* (Edinburgh: Polygon/Birlinn, [2002] 2008)

Kelman, James, 'Introduction' to Hugh Savage, *Born Up a Close: Memoirs of a Brigton Boy* (Glendaruel, Scotland: Argyll Publishing, 2006), pp. 9–65. [History of Glasgow radicalism in the twentieth century]

Kelman, James, 'Afterword' to *An Old Pub Near the Angel and Other Stories* (Edinburgh: Polygon/Birlinn, 2007), pp. 121–83. [Essential autobiographical source]

Kelman, James, 'Quick notes on twelve plays', unpublished, undated. [Reflections and suggestions for prospective directors]

Kelman Interviews

Anderson, Darran, 'The War Against Silence: An Interview with James Kelman', *3:AM Magazine*, 20 November 2008, www.3ammagazine.com/3am/the-war-against-silence-an-interview-with-james-kelman/ (accessed 30 August 2009)

Clark, William, 'A Conversation with James Kelman', *Variant* 12 (2001), www.variant.randomstate.org/12ts/Kelman.html (accessed 30 August 2009)

Gardiner, Michael, 'James Kelman Interviewed', *Scottish Studies Review* 5.1 (Spring 2004), pp. 101–15

Kelman, James, 'K is for culture . . . Interview with Scottish writer James Kelman', *Scottish Trade Union Review* 68 (January–February 1995), pp. 24–9

McAlpine, Joan, 'How the Booker bust James Kelman', *The Times*, 5 April 2009

McLean, Duncan, 'James Kelman Interviewed', *Edinburgh Review* 71 (1985), pp. 64–80

McNeill, Kirsty, 'Interview with James Kelman', *Chapman* 57 (1989), pp. 1–9

Toremans, Tom, 'Interview with Alasdair Gray and James Kelman', *Contemporary Literature* 44.4 (2003), pp. 565–86

Vericat, Fabio, 'An Interview with James Kelman', *Barcelona Review* 28 (2002), www.barcelonareview.com/28/e_jk.htm (accessed 30 August 2009)

Criticism

Ahmad, Dora (ed.), *Rotten English: A Literary Anthology* (London: W.W. Norton, 2007)

Ashcroft, Bill, *Caliban's Voice: The Transformation of English in Post-Colonial Literatures* (London: Routledge, 2009)

Ashcroft, Bill, Gareth Griffiths, and Helen Tiffin, *The Empire Writes Back*, 2nd edn (London: Routledge, 2002)

Baker, Simon, '"Wee Stories With a Working-Class Theme": The Reimagining of Urban Realism in the Fiction of James Kelman' in *Studies in Scottish Fiction: 1945 to the Present*, ed. Susanne Hagemann (Frankfurt am Main: Peter Lang, 1996), pp. 235–50

Barnes, Hugh, 'Down and out in Glesga low life', *The Times*, 2 May 1991

Barthes, Roland, *Writing Degree Zero*, trans. Annette Lavers and Colin Smith (New York: Hill & Wang, [1953] 1968)

Beaumont, Matthew (ed.), *Adventures in Realism* (Oxford: Blackwell, 2007)

Beckett, Samuel, *The Beckett Trilogy: Molloy, Malone Dies, The Unnameable* (London: Picador, 1979)

Benjamin, Walter, *Illuminations*, ed. Hannah Arendt, trans. Harry Zohn (New York: Schocken/Harcourt Brace Jovanovich, 1968)

Benjamin, Walter, *The Arcades Project*, trans. Howard Eiland and Kevin McLaughlin (Cambridge, MA: Belknap Press of Harvard University, 1999)

Bhabha, Homi, *The Location of Culture* (London: Routledge, 1994)

Black, Ian, 'Kelman lines up his next shot,' *The Sunday Times*, 16 October 1994

Boehmer, Elleke, *Colonial and Postcolonial Literature: Migrant Metaphors* (Oxford: Oxford University Press, 1995)

Brathwaite, Edward Kamau, *History of the Voice* (London: New Beacon, 1984)

Camus, Albert, *The Outsider*, trans. Joseph Laredo (Harmondsworth: Penguin, 1987)

Casanova, Pascale, *The World Republic of Letters*, trans. M. B. DeBevoise (Cambridge, MA: Harvard University Press, 2004)

Chomsky, Noam, *Problems of Knowledge and Freedom* (London: Fontana, 1972)

Corbett, John, *Language and Scottish Literature* (Edinburgh: Edinburgh University Press, 1997)

Craig, Cairns, 'Resisting Arrest: James Kelman', in *The Scottish Novel Since the Seventies*, eds Gavin Wallace and Randall Stevenson (Edinburgh: Edinburgh University Press, 1993), pp. 99–114

Craig, Cairns, *Out of History: Narrative Paradigms in Scottish and English Culture* (Edinburgh: Polygon, 1996)

Craig, Cairns, *The Modern Scottish Novel: Narrative and the National Imagination* (Edinburgh: Edinburgh University Press, 1999)

Crumey, Andrew, '"And the Judges Said . . .": Tired Polemic From a Master of His Tedium', *Scotland on Sunday*, 21 April 2002

Daly, Macdonald, 'Your Average Working Kelman', *Cencrastus* 46 (1993), pp. 14–16

Deleuze, Gilles and Félix Guattari, *Kafka: Toward a Minor Literature*, trans. Dana Polan (Minneapolis, MN: University of Minnesota Press, [1975] 1986)

Dostoevksy, Fyodor, *Notes from Underground*, trans. Jessie Coulson (Harmondsworth: Penguin, [1864] 1972)

Dunn, Douglas, 'I'm right, and good, you're bad', *Times Literary Supplement*, 1 January 1993

Eagleton, Terry, 'James Kelman', in *Figures of Dissent: Critical Essays on Fish, Spivak, Zizek and Others* (London: Verso, 2003), pp. 263–5

Engledow, Sarah, 'Studying Form: the Off-the-Page Politics of *A Chancer*', *Edinburgh Review* 108 (2001), pp. 69–84

Fielding, Penny, *Writing and Orality: Nationality, Culture, and Nineteenth-Century Scottish Fiction* (Oxford: Clarendon, 1996)

Freeman, Alan, 'The Humanist's Dilemma: A Polemic Against Kelman's Polemics', *Edinburgh Review* 108 (2001), pp. 28–40

Frow, John, *Cultural Studies and Cultural Value* (Oxford: Oxford University Press, 1995)

Gardiner, Michael, *From Trocchi to Trainspotting: Scottish Critical Theory Since 1960* (Edinburgh: Edinburgh University Press, 2006)

Goring, Rosemary, 'Smashing the state of creative writing,' *The Herald* (Glasgow), 11 August 2007

Guillory, John, *Cultural Capital: the Problem of Literary Canon Formation* (Chicago, IL: University of Chicago Press, 1993)

Hagemann, Susanne, 'Postcolonial Translation Studies and James Kelman's *Translated Accounts*', *Scottish Studies Review* 6.1 (2005), pp. 74–83

Hames, Scott, 'Dogged Masculinities: Male Subjectivity and Socialist Despair in Kelman and McIlvanney', *Scottish Studies Review* 8.1 (2007), pp. 67–87

Hames, Scott, 'Eyeless in Glasgow: James Kelman's Existential Milton', *Contemporary Literature* 50.3 (2009), pp. 496–527

Hobsbaum, Philip, 'The Glasgow Group', *Edinburgh Review* 80.1 (1988), pp. 58–63

Huggan, Graham, 'Prizing "Otherness": A Short History of the Booker', *Studies in the Novel* 29.3 (1997), pp. 412–33

Jackson, Ellen-Raïssa and Willy Maley, 'Committing to Kelman: the Art of Integrity and the Politics of Dissent', *Edinburgh Review* 108 (2001), pp. 22–7

Jameson, Fredric, *The Prison-House of Language* (London: Princeton University Press, 1972)

Jenkins, Simon, 'An Expletive of a Winner', *The Times*, 15 October 1994

Joyce, James, *Ulysses: The 1922 Text*, ed. Jeri Johnson (Oxford: Oxford University Press, 1993)

Kafka, Franz, *The Complete Stories*, ed. Nahum H. Glatzer (New York: Schocken, 1971)

Kelly, Aaron, 'James Kelman and the Deterritorialisation of Power', in *The Edinburgh Companion to Contemporary Scottish Literature*, ed. Berthold Schoene (Edinburgh: Edinburgh University Press, 2007), pp. 175–83

Kirk, John, 'Figuring the Dispossessed: Images of the Urban Working Class in the Writing of James Kelman', *English* 48 (1999), pp. 101–16

Klaus, H. Gustav, 'James Kelman: A Voice from the Lower Depths of Thatcherite Britain', *London Magazine* (August/September 1989), pp. 39–48

154 FURTHER READING

Klaus, H. Gustav, 'Kelman for Beginners', *Journal of the Short Story in English* 22 (1994), pp. 127–35

Klaus, H. Gustav, *James Kelman* (Tavistock: Northcote House, 2004)

Knights, Ben, *Writing Masculinities: Male Narratives in Twentieth-Century Fiction* (Basingstoke: Macmillan, 1999)

Kövesi, Simon, *James Kelman* (Manchester: Manchester University Press, 2007)

Leonard, Tom, *Intimate Voices: Selected Work 1965–1983* (Exbourne, Devon: Etruscan, [1984] 2003)

Lukács, Georg, *The Meaning of Contemporary Realism*, trans. John and Necke Mander (London: Merlin, 1963)

Lukács, Georg, *Writer and Critic*, trans. Arthur Kahn (London: Merlin, 1970)

Macarthur, J. D., 'The Narrative Voice in James Kelman's *The Burn*', *Studies in English Literature* 71 (1995), pp. 181–95

Macarthur, J. D., *Claiming Your Portion of Space: A Study of the Short Stories of James Kelman* (Tokyo: Hokuseido, 2007)

MacCabe, Colin, *James Joyce and the Revolution of the Word* (London: Macmillan, 1978)

Macdonald, Graeme, 'Writing Claustrophobia: Zola and Kelman', *Bulletin of the Emile Zola Society*, March 1996 (Glasgow: University of Glasgow French and German Publications)

Maley, Willy, 'Denizens, citizens, tourists and others: marginality and mobility in the writings of James Kelman and Irvine Welsh', in *City Visions*, eds David Bell and Azzedine Haddour (Harlow: Longman, 2000), pp. 60–72

March, Cristie L., *Rewriting Scotland: Welsh, McLean, Banks, Galloway and Kennedy* (Manchester: Manchester University Press, 2002)

McGlynn, Mary, '"Middle-Class Wankers" and Working-class Texts: The Critics and James Kelman', *Contemporary Literature* 43.1 (2002), pp. 50–84

McIlvanney, Liam, 'The Politics of Narrative in the Post-war Scottish Novel', in *On Modern British Fiction*, ed. Zachary Leader (Oxford: Oxford University Press, 2002), pp. 181–208

McMillan, Neil, 'Wilting, or the "Poor Wee Boy Syndrome": Kelman and Masculinity', *Edinburgh Review* 108 (2001), pp. 41–55

McMunnigall, Alan and Gerard Carruthers, 'Locating Kelman: Glasgow, Scotland and the Commitment to Place', *Edinburgh Review* 108 (2001), pp. 56–8

McNeill, Dougal, '"Edging Back Into Awareness": *How Late it Was, How Late*, Form, and the Utopian Demand', *COLLOQUY text theory critique* 15 (2008) [http://colloquy.monash.edu.au/issue015/mcneill.pdf]

Meek, James, 'Dead not Deid', *London Review of Books* 30.10 (2008), pp. 5–8

Milne, Drew, 'Dialectics of Urbanity', in *Writing Region and Nation: A Special Number of the Swansea Review*, eds James A. Davies et al. (Swansea: Department of English, University of Wales, 1994), pp. 393–407

Milne, Drew, 'Broken English: James Kelman's *Translated Accounts*', *Edinburgh Review* 108 (2001), pp. 106–15

Mugglestone, Lynda, *Talking Proper: The Rise of Accent as Social Symbol*, 2nd edn (London: Oxford University Press, 2003)

Nicoll, Laurence, 'Gogol's Overcoat: Kelman *Resartus*', *Edinburgh Review* 108 (2001), pp. 116–22

Nicoll, Laurence, 'Facticity, or Something Like That: The Novels of James Kelman', in *The Contemporary British Novel Since 1980*, eds James Acheson and Sarah C. E. Ross (London: Palgrave, 2006), pp. 59–69

Pitchford, Nicola, 'How Late It Was for England: James Kelman's Scottish Booker Prize', *Contemporary Literature* 41.1 (2000), pp. 693–725

Robbe-Grillet, Alain, *For a New Novel*, trans. Richard Howard (Evanston, IL: Northwestern University Press, [1963] 1989)

Saro-Wiwa, Ken, *Sozaboy: A Novel in Rotten English* (London: Longman, [1985] 1994)

Sartre, Jean-Paul, *What is Literature?*, trans. Bernard Frechtman (London: Routledge, 1967)

Selvon, Sam, *The Lonely Londoners* (London: Longman, [1956] 1985)

Shklovsky, Viktor, *Theory of Prose*, trans. Benjamin Sher (Normal, IL: Dalkey Archive, [1929] 1990)

Smith, Barbara Herrnstein, *Contingencies of Value: Alternative Perspectives for Critical Theory* (London: Harvard University Press, 1988)

Spinks, Lee, '"In Juxtaposition to Which?": Narrative, System and Subjectivity in the Fiction of James Kelman,' *Edinburgh Review* 108 (2001), pp. 85–105

Talib, Ismail, *The Language of Postcolonial Literatures* (London: Routledge, 2002)

Todd, Richard, *Consuming Fictions: The Booker Prize and Fiction in Britain Today* (London: Bloomsbury, 1998)

Tutuola, Amos, *The Palm-Wine Drinkard* (London: Faber & Faber, [1952] 1977)

Vice, Sue, *Introducing Bakhtin* (Manchester: Manchester University Press, 1997)

Watson, Roderick, 'Alien Voices from the Street: Demotic Modernism in Modern Scots Writing', in *The Yearbook of English Studies*, ed. Andrew Gurr (London: Maney, 1995), pp. 141–55

Watson, Roderick, 'Postcolonial Subjects? Language, Narrative Authority and Class in Contemporary Scottish Culture', *Hungarian Journal of English and American Studies* 4.1–2 (1998), pp. 21–38

Whyte, Christopher, 'Masculinities in Contemporary Scottish Fiction', *Forum for Modern Language Studies* 34.3 (1998), pp. 274–85

Wood, James, 'In Defence of Kelman', *The Guardian*, 25 October 1994

Wroe, Nicholas, 'Glasgow Kith', *The Guardian*, 2 June 2001

Zola, Émile, *The Experimental Novel and Other Essays*, trans. Belle M. Sherman, (New York: Haskell House, [1880] 1964)

Notes on Contributors

David Archibald teaches in the Department of Theatre, Film and Television Studies at the University of Glasgow. His research interests lie mainly in film and he is currently completing a monograph on the Spanish Civil War in Cinema. He has also published material on various aspects of Scotland's cultural and political landscape.

Peter Boxall is Professor of English at the University of Sussex. He has published widely on modern and contemporary literature. Recent books include *Don DeLillo: The Possibility of Fiction* (2006) and *Since Beckett: Contemporary Writing in the Wake of Modernism* (2009). He is currently editor of *Textual Practice*.

Mia Carter is an Associate Professor of English and Distinguished Teaching Professor at the University of Texas at Austin. Her fields of specialisation are British Studies, Imperial Studies, Modernism, Cultural Studies, and European and World Cinema.

Cairns Craig is Director of the AHRC Centre for Scottish and Irish Studies at the University of Aberdeen. Author of *Out of History* (1996), *The Modern Scottish Novel* (1999) and *Associationism and the Literary Imagination* (2007), he was general editor of Aberdeen University Press's four-volume *History of Scottish Literature* (1987–9).

Michael Gardiner is Assistant Professor in the Department of English and Comparative Literature at the University of Warwick. His publications include *From Trocchi to Trainspotting: Scottish Critical Theory Since 1960* (2006), *The Cultural Roots of British Devolution* (2004) and one book of fiction, *Escalator* (2006).

Scott Hames is Lecturer in English Studies at the University of Stirling. He has written widely on Kelman, and will soon publish a monograph on

Kelman's literary vernacular. He co-edits the *International Journal of Scottish Literature*.

Adrian Hunter is Senior Lecturer in English Studies at the University of Stirling. He is the author of, among other things, *The Cambridge Introduction to the Short Story in English*.

Carole Jones is Lecturer in English at the University of Edinburgh. Her research engages with issues of gender and sexuality in contemporary writing, and she has published widely on Scottish fiction. She is the author of *Disappearing Men: Gender Disorientation in Scottish Fiction, 1979–1999* (2009).

Mary McGlynn is Associate Professor of English at Baruch College, City University of New York. She writes about contemporary Irish and Scottish fiction and popular culture. Her book, *Narratives of Class in New Irish and Scottish Fiction*, was published by Palgrave Macmillan in 2008.

Laurence Nicoll has taught at the universities of Edinburgh and Aberdeen. He is currently working on a study of Robin Jenkins' *The Cone-Gatherers*.

Paul Shanks is a Research Fellow at the AHRC Centre for Irish and Scottish Studies at Aberdeen and is interested in literary and cultural overlaps in twentieth-century Irish, Scottish and European writing. He is currently preparing a monograph introduction to Samuel Beckett as part of the Aberdeen Introductions to Irish and Scottish Culture series.

Index